SONOMA COUNTY

WINE LIBRARY

The Good Life Guide to Enjoying Wine

RAY JOHNSON

THE WRITERS' COLLECTIVE™

Independent Books for Independent Readers

The Good Life Guide to Enjoying Wine
© 2006 by Ray Johnson

Interior Design: Barbara Hodge
Cover Design: Barbara Hodge
Illustrations: Linda Johnson
Cover Photography: Jim Ross
Executive Editor: Sarah Sperry
Editor: Mary Evely
Proof Reader: Sonja Hyams

ISBN-13: 978-1-59411-081-8
ISBN-10: 1-59411-081-6

LCCN: 2004095577

Printed in the United States of America
10 9 8 7 6 5 4 3 2 1

Published by The Writers' Collective™ ♦ Cranston, Rhode Island

CONTENTS

Acknowledgments

For Linda, my steadfast source of encouragement.

I thank David Hehman, Sarah Sperry, and Sam Truitt for inviting me to write this book and encouraging it along the way.

Thanks to many colleagues, who each took a section of the book for technical review. To Wilfred Wong, Elizabeth Slater, David Jones, and Robin Calkins, special thanks for reading the entire work.

Thanks as well to the friends and students who sweated a hot day in the sun to create a glowing cover: Brad Calkins, Robin Calkins, Greg Chatfield, Catherine Gutfreund, Sarah Hehman, Hilary Hoeber, Paul Hulsman, Ken Hunt, Suzanne Madsen, Hillary Reck, Ronald Taylor, and Ruth DiDonna Taylor. Special thanks to Robin Calkins and the team at Kendall-Jackson's Wine Center for handling the logistics and creating the venue, and to Linda Johnson for cooking up a gourmet picnic and assisting our favorite professional photographer, Jim Ross.

INTRODUCTION

How do you get girls to notice you in college? Order a bottle of wine in a restaurant. It was enough to get me hooked, and after I started waiting tables it became clear that the easiest way to build my check average was to sell wine. I went deeper into the subject, traveling to Europe and tasting regularly, and after a few years of drinking rare and expensive vintages became a wine snob.

Fortunately I came back to earth while working at the Christian Brothers Winery in the Napa Valley, where thousands of visitors from around the country were as delighted with their White Zinfandel as with their critically acclaimed Cabernet Sauvignon. The experience cured me of my snobbery and helped me to appreciate the pleasure that even a simple wine can give us. In 1998 I started teaching, and discovered that in my classes and wine tastings students asked the same questions I heard so many years ago. This guide is a compilation of my answers, and will help new *enophiles* (wine lovers) to develop confidence in their own taste while learning where to find favorites in restaurants and shops. Old pros will discover helpful tips on everything from serving to storing to giving the gift of wine, while cutting through the pretensions that are sometimes associated with fine vintages.

Most importantly, this guide will prove to sophisticated wine lovers and newcomers alike that the keys to enjoying great wines are already in their mouths, and that wine tasting is its own reward on the path of the Good Life.

One

LEARNING WHAT
YOU LIKE

If it sounds good, it is good.
— Duke Ellington

TASTING THE GAMUT

Do you have to study chocolate to know whether or not you like it? No way. But you do need to taste it. That's how you discovered that you liked milk chocolate over bittersweet or one brand over another.

Like chocolate, wine comes in many flavors, and many brands can taste dramatically different. To discover what styles you like best, you need to taste the gamut. In this chapter, you will explore wines from seven broad categories to nail down what you like best. This short study will give you the solid footing you need for engaging any retail wine clerk or restaurant sommelier.

Using the shopping list provided, purchase a wine from each style to discern if you like them all or just a few. You might share the cost and shopping with a group of friends and taste the wines together. You can easily share the bottles among twelve people at one tasting. One bottle or a half bottle should suffice for each style of wine listed. Plan on spending $50–$100 for the entire group of wines, depending on your selections and the competitiveness of the market where you shop.

The wines provided in this list are suggested because they are generally easy to find and economical. I list multiple brands for purchase suggestions in case your store has limited selection. I'm not looking to impress you with my knowledge of artisan producers, who make only a few cases of wine that only the FBI can locate. Just buy these more mainstream wines to run through the game. I'd also ignore vintages at this point and ask for help if you can't find something. You'll also notice that some of the suggested producers make more than one version of the wine I recommend tasting: e.g., Blackstone produces several different Merlots. You'll hit the target style buying any of them found in most grocery stores. Just pick what best suits your budget and save the big money for buying the kinds of wine you find that you love after this exploration is over.

In all of the classes I've taught encompassing boatloads of wine topics, nothing empowers the participants more than defining and articulating what they like. You can do this process as quickly or as methodically as you please. A quick run through the styles will help define your tastes. A slower, more methodical walk will give you more language for describing what you like best. So don't skip this chance to do some tasting. Go to it!

SHOPPING LIST

TYPE/STYLE	PURCHASE SUGGESTIONS
VERY DRY WHITE	❑ *Geyser Peak Sauvignon Blanc* ❑ *St. Supéry Sauvignon Blanc* ❑ *Dry Creek Fumé Blanc*
RICH WHITE	❑ *Kendall-Jackson Chardonnay* ❑ *Meridian Chardonnay* ❑ *Benziger Chardonnay*
LIGHTLY SWEET WHITE	❑ *Beringer White Zinfandel* ❑ *Fetzer Riesling* ❑ *Fetzer Gewürztraminer*
LIGHT AND SOFT RED	❑ *La Crema Pinot Noir* ❑ *Forest Glen Merlot* ❑ *Blackstone Merlot*
HEAVIER STRUCTURED RED	❑ *Beringer Cabernet Sauvignon* ❑ *Benziger Cabernet Sauvignon* ❑ *Bogle Petite Sirah*
WHITE DESSERT	❑ *Bonny Doon Muscat Vin de Glacière* ❑ *Quady Essensia* ❑ *Sutter Home Moscato*
RED DESSERT	❑ *Quady Elysium* ❑ *Christian Brothers Ruby Port* ❑ *Fonseca Port*

Note: Remember you only need to purchase one wine for each of the seven categories mentioned. Notice how the wines in the Purchase Suggestions column are written. Most American wines you'll encounter are named after the grape and winery that made them. For example, Geyser Peak Sauvignon Blanc is a wine made from the Sauvignon Blanc grape at a winery named Geyser Peak.

Here's a cheat sheet for deciphering many American labels:

- Sauvignon Blanc, Roussanne, and Pinot Grigio grapes often make dry white wine.
- Chardonnay, Viognier, and Sémillon grapes often make rich white wine.
- Riesling, Gewürztraminer, and Chenin Blanc grapes often make lightly sweet white wine.
- Merlot, Gamay, and Pinot Noir grapes often make light and soft red wine.
- Cabernet Sauvignon, Barbera, and Petite Sirah grapes often make heavier structured red wine.

In Chapter 10, Wine Primer, I describe lots more choices of each wine style and crossover varietals like Dry Riesling and sweet Cabernet Sauvignon.

THE SET UP

Taste the wines alone or with some trusted friends. By "trusted," I mean people who are open-minded and won't pooh-pooh your opinions. In my classes it often happens that somebody in a group will try to appoint himself (it is most often a "him") as the expert and proceed to tell the others what's good and what's not. You don't need this kind of arrogance in the room when you're enjoying and discovering what styles of wine you like best.

Try the wines in any order over as many nights as you wish. You might taste one or two of the wines during the course of each evening. First taste them solo, and then drink them with your dinner and notice how the taste of the wines changes with whatever you're eating. Don't be concerned with wine and food pairing—we'll explore this later. For now, just taste the wines alone and with whatever foods are on hand.

Or, if you're in the mood for a festive night, host a tasting for some friends. Try all seven styles of wine in the sequence on the shopping list. To set up, have a wineglass available for each person attending. You don't need to rinse the glasses with water between tastes until you get to the dessert white. Before tasting that one, change glasses or give your current one a good rinse to avoid making a rosé with the previous red wine.

Give each person an additional cup for spitting or dumping their excess wine. Spitting can seem awkward, but, believe it or not, you can deeply experience a wine without swallowing it—just roll it around in your mouth. Whether you spit or not, you'll want to dump out the wines that didn't appeal to you and go back for seconds on your favorites.

Some nibbles would be nice: a bit of cheese, cold meats, hummus, crackers, cookies, and chocolates. It's not necessary to eat, it's just more fun. At professional judgings, we'll taste dozens of wines without a bite. This changes when we judge heavy, tannic red wines, but for a tasting of seven wines, food is an enhancement, not a necessity.

Give each guest a glass of water to drink, put a carafe or pot on the table in case the spit cups fill up, chill your whites in the refrigerator, and you're ready to go.

A Tasting Tutorial

Pour an ounce or two of the first wine in a clear glass and tilt the glass against a white background. Notice the wine's tint or hue. White wines range from a yellow, sometimes greenish, color to shades of gold and amber. Red wines range from a purple, sometimes blackish, color through shades of red to tawny and brown. Note the depth of color or concentration, ranging from transparent to opaque. Is there any sediment or other matter?

Next, swirl the wine in the glass and take a forceful sniff; don't be bashful. Notice the aroma (any odor derived from the grape itself) and the bouquet (any odor derived from the fermentation or aging of the wine). What does the smell remind you of? It could be one thing or many, especially as the wine spends more time in the glass. Note the intensity of the odors you experience: gobs of strawberries, a hint of oak, a dab of butter.

Take a small sip and let your whole palate experience the wine. Draw a breath across the wine in your mouth and note the taste sensations and their intensity. Below is a list adapted from Michael Broadbent's *Pocket Guide to Winetasting* that most succinctly explains the sensations that you'll experience:

- *Flavor.* Does the wine remind you of another food or beverage?
- *Sweetness* is best perceived at the front tip of the tongue. Notice the distinction between sweetness and the fruit flavors of the wine.
- *Acidity.* Is it super-sour like lemon juice, flat like water, or somewhere in between?
- *Tannin.* A plain cup of very strong tea provides a dramatic example. In wine, tannin can exhibit itself as a velvety coating inside your mouth, a mouth-puckering, bitter dryness or something in between.
- *Body* is the weight of the wine. Is it light like water or heavy like a Piña Colada?
- More tactile sensations describe the feeling of the wine in your mouth. "Creamy" has a positive connotation; "burning" isn't so popular.
- Do you feel that the wine has balance? Are the components in harmony? If the components were bars on a graph, do they hit the same heights? This is very subjective, so don't feel shy about asserting your opinion.

Note the sensations that remain after you spit or swallow the wine. Remember the relative length of these sensations. It's such a pleasure when the flavors you enjoy linger on and on.

Using the chart provided on the following page, write some concluding thoughts, judgments, or observations. Which wines did you like? Which wines did you hate? Comments could include your feelings about the wine's relative value and whether or not you would buy it. There's space for up to three wines per style and more room at the end of the book for the wines you sample down the road.

THE ULTIMATE TASTE TEST

TYPE/STYLE   **COMMENTS**

VERY DRY WHITE

Name of wine:

Name of wine:

Name of wine:

RICH WHITE

Name of wine:

Name of wine:

Name of wine:

LIGHTLY SWEET WHITE

Name of wine:

Name of wine:

Name of wine:

LIGHT AND SOFT RED

Name of wine:

Name of wine:

Name of wine:

8

THE GOOD LIFE GUIDE TO ENJOYING WINE

THE ULTIMATE TASTE TEST

TYPE/STYLE **COMMENTS**

HEAVIER STRUCTURED RED

Name of wine:

Name of wine:

Name of wine:

WHITE DESSERT

Name of wine:

Name of wine:

Name of wine:

RED DESSERT

Name of wine:

Name of wine:

Name of wine:

Describing What You Like

Make your notes about the wines like a stream-of-consciousness novel in the chart provided. Just let the adjectives come out—no editing. The advantage to tasting with an uninhibited friend is that the adjectives can really roll like a brainstorming session. The disadvantage comes if your friend is uptight and worried about getting the descriptions "right."

Not only is the notion of "right descriptions" flawed, there is little chance that anyone else can know exactly what your grandmother's attic smelled like. And then there's the problem of memory. It's hard to remember how something tasted or smelled. And it's even harder to put the words to those memories. Sometimes the taste and smell of a wine is so familiar, yet the words are out of reach. Does it matter? I don't think so.

This is why a *trusted* friend is so helpful when tasting. How often I've overheard this script:

Sally: "I smell strawberries."

Dick: "I don't smell that!" (Translate as: "That's wrong: That's not in there.")

I think this attitude is rubbish. If you smell baby diapers in a wine that smells like strawberries to me, that's OK. The winery isn't putting either in the wine. What we're really doing is using metaphors to describe what the wine reminds us of. It's this discussion and sharing that's fun—not getting the "right" answer and a gold star from the teacher.

Just about anything is fair game with wine descriptions. About the only two words I try to avoid are "bad" and "good." It's easy to say a wine is bad when we don't like it and very easy to say it's good when we do like it. Even experts are susceptible to the same biases at professional wine judgings. If I like the flavors of a wine, I tend to score it higher. I'm only human.

Two

RETAIL STRATEGIES

A healthy male adult bore consumes each year one and a half times his own weight in other people's patience.
— John Updike

CHASING A BRAND

You've done the hard work, tasting the wine, nailing down what you like best, and creating your own notes along the way. But while a record of the particular brands of wine you like has great value, it can also be a trap.

When I worked in retail, there were many occasions when a customer would enter with a wine label, inquiring about a wine they loved. More often than not, the wine was gone, sold-out, or unavailable at any price. After explaining this, they would leave and travel onto the next shop, searching in vain for a high they couldn't possibly duplicate. While Cheerios and Frosted Flakes will always be on the shelf, that 2001 Chateau Chez Ray Merlot won't.

However, if you can describe the *type* or *style* of wine you like, you can work with a competent salesclerk to get something you'll enjoy. And if the salesclerk has tasted any of the particular wines you like, they'll have an even clearer picture of what makes you smile. For example, "I like the Geyser Peak Sauvignon Blanc, but more importantly, I like very dry white wine. What do you have in the ballpark?"

By understanding the broader types or styles of wine, you'll avoid the pitfall of chasing a particular brand of wine you can't find. Keeping some notes on the wines you've tasted, as in The Ultimate Taste Test, creates a translation book—a version of the Berlitz French-English pocketbook you might carry to France. With your translation guide in hand and a knowledgeable wine clerk, you can rest assured that you will always find a satisfying bottle.

IN THE SUPERMARKET

If you live in an area where you can buy wine in a grocery store, you're probably blessed with access to competitively priced wine. You will not always find bargains in the grocery store, but in an area where there are more choices beyond specialty wine shops, everyone selling wine tries to maintain the appearance of friendly prices.

Many of the large supermarkets stock and display their wine according to a schematic developed at the corporate level. Notice how the wine is organized as you stand in front of the shelves. Perhaps the most expensive wine is on the top shelf and the cheapest requires bending to the floor. Most likely the wines are categorized by the grapes from which they were made, all of the Chardonnay in one section, say. Perhaps the imports are grouped by the countries and regions from which they come.

Staring back at you, eye-level in the middle of the Chardonnay section, may be the bestsellers of the store. Markets know the tendency of their shoppers to look at the middle of the section they are shopping. They also know your tendency to *trade up* to the right. When you're next shopping for Martini ingredients, notice how the vodka or gin is arranged. If the store carries three sizes, they're probably arranged left to right, smallest and cheapest on the left, moving up in size to the right. Since we read this way in the West, we tend to see what's to the right and often splurge on the big one. Like Tide and Cheerios, we imagine that the larger size is a better value. And sometimes that is true when the smaller bottles aren't on special.

The merchandise on promo is where the bargains are. Contrary to many after-season clothing sales, much of the wine on sale is not merchandise that has to be shifted at the end of a season. A winery might offer a price break to encourage product movement at any time, which is passed on via the wholesaler to the retailer. The shop may be able to make its typical margin of profit, and we benefit with lower prices. Wines merchandised and featured at a discount are the way to go if they are what you like.

In contrast, buying regular-priced merchandise off the shelf is seldom a deal. Margins are often higher as are prices. Think of it like the casinos in Las Vegas: frequent payouts at the fringes tempt you toward the inside where you're less likely to emerge a winner. Similarly with the supermarket wine department, great sales are on the perimeter and higher regular prices are centered on the shelves.

This underlines one of the big minuses of grocery store wine buying—everyday merchandise is often priced too high. Another big drawback is that the selection is typically safe, sticking to the best sellers of every category, thus breeding a chicken and egg story. Consumers purchase the best sellers, reinforcing those wines as the best sellers, and these wines are promoted on special, making them most visible on display and again, the top sellers.

The other challenge comes back to customer service. Though the butcher in the meat department may like Cabernet Sauvignon, he probably does not taste dozens of wines a week. Some stores will pay the money to have a knowledgeable wine person on staff, especially the upmarket stores with a gourmet focus. And if they are there, solicit their advice. You might ask for recommendations that taste similar to the particular type or style of wine you like. Or, ask for a wine that offers the best value for the money or for something that fits your wine budget.

Shopping by the Grape

If the buyer is swamped or absent, here are some buying tips to help narrow down your choices:

· Stay aware of the styles of wine you liked best
· Keep track of the producers, the wineries that hit the mark for you, delivering wines of the type you like
· Have a price point in mind before you shop
· Ignore vintages
· Ignore wine regions

If you're just getting started, you may only have a few wines and wineries on your short list of favorites, and there is a chance nothing in the store matches your list. What next? A somewhat rough but useful guide is to shop by grape. Let's say you loved the very dry white, a Sauvignon Blanc. You might try another Sauvignon Blanc from a different winery.

The reason this approach is rough is because of the diverse winemaking techniques that will influence the taste of a given wine. Some Sauvignon Blancs are actually rich and buttery, as are many Chardonnays. Likewise not all Chardonnays are created equal. Some are crisp and acidic.

It can be quite confusing, but sometimes the back label on the bottle will provide some clues. Phrases like "stainless steel fermentation" and "no malolactic" often correlate with dry, acidic white wines. Descriptors like "buttery," "full malolactic fermentation," and "oak fermentation and aging" often portend a richer style of white wine. Residual sugar levels at or above .5 percent start to indicate noticeable sweetness.

Despite these tips and indicators, it's really impossible to know what to expect before you open the bottle. Some oaky Chardonnays are quite bracing with acidity, tasting rich and dry at the same time. We can narrow the field quite a bit when shopping by grape, but it won't replace tasting that wine or talking with somebody who has.

In the Wine Shop

If you have a wine shop or a beverage superstore nearby, you absolutely must visit. Like other retail venues, these stores run the gamut from rude to friendly and cheap to chic. Some specialize, some have it all, and I generally judge them by price and service, both traits of equal importance. Appearance and atmosphere are only worth considering in three regards: high temperatures, sunshine, and mess. Indoor temperatures reminiscent of Arizona in the summer and streams of sunshine on window displays should cause grave concern, as high heat and sunshine are very hard on wine. And a pigsty on the sales floor might reflect a similar disregard for the wine stored in the backroom. Though more durable than milk, wine is a food product that requires some care in handling.

The décor might range from upmarket brass and oak to stacks of cardboard cases on a concrete floor. Neither milieu makes the wine taste better, and you can bet that your spending at the posh venue is helping to finance its patina. Whether a dump or a palace, the friendliest wine shops can still feel intimidating. Seldom will the place be jammed with shoppers, so there's less opportunity to shop anonymously. Wine retailers are passionate about wine and love to talk about it, so within minutes of arriving, you'll probably find someone eager to help even when you just want to amble silently.

The pluses of a good wine store more than offset the step out of anonymous shopping. There's a better chance you'll find experienced staff with diverse wine experience. If you absolutely want to shop for high-end wine, this is where the selection will be best. And the big secret is that if you want to shop for the most interesting cheap wine, this is the place where you'll find the greatest selection.

While wine shops harbor a bigger selection of triple digit wines than most grocery stores, the buyers are also keen to find good, inexpensive wine. Anybody with a big wallet can buy Dom Pérignon, but it takes more effort to find tasty wines at bargain prices, and wine store managers and buyers live for this treasure hunt. Most of them are bright people who passed up high paying careers to live out their dream of working in the wine industry. So, if you're already spending $4–$10 per bottle, the best opportunity for value is in an unpretentious wine shop.

THE TRUSTED ADVISOR

Beyond the dollar benefits, you can establish a personal relationship with a trusted advisor—someone who learns what you like and can recommend alternatives as you explore the world of wine. Finding that trusted advisor takes some doing. You have to seek out the real people in wine—the truly service-oriented staff. Along the way, you'll certainly encounter some of these characters:

- *The snob:* They know what's good and can't understand why anyone would drink White Zinfandel, even if it restored a youthful complexion. Their pretentiousness is almost painful to listen to, like your friend who waxes ad infinitum about his new Beemer.
- *The teacher:* They want to broaden your perspective by introducing you to lots of wine that you won't like. If you've tasted the seven types of wine from the Shopping List, you've done the groundwork. You also don't have time to listen to somebody who wants to tell you everything they know about wine. Often, it's just too much information.
- *The elevator:* While they accept what you like, they are determined to raise your awareness, educate you on what they think is better than what you like. This attitude presupposes that there is a destination to wine appreciation and that you've been blessed with meeting the gatekeeper at the beginning of the long staircase of increasingly sophisticated taste.

The truly giving, service-minded people are my favorite. They listen to what you want before even hinting at a suggestion. They translate what you like and want into something in the shop's inventory. They also respect your budget. And when you return, you're asked what you thought of the wine you took home last and how to fine-tune your next selection. This gem of a person doesn't take it as a personal affront when you don't like a wine they suggest and they don't consider it a reflection on their knowledge. It's like speaking with someone from France when your native tongue is English. It can take a few tries to really know what each other means by subjectively understood words like "dry."

VINTAGES

Vintages are such a low priority that I don't even recommend reading about them for the first ten years of wine drinking, which may seem completely at odds with all of the ink you've seen spilled on this topic over the years. Here's a brief synopsis of what you need to know.

The term *vintage* refers to the harvest of grapes from a particular year. A wine's vintage is particularly important, to winemakers and grape growers, in places where it is difficult to ripen grapes and where the weather can be unpredictable. Yet, as Johannes Selbach told me when comparing the 2000 and 2001 vintages in Germany's Mosel-Saar-Ruwer, "In 2001 we had very pure, ripe fruit. The 2000 harvest separated the men from the boys; it was tough and the vintage required good selection." This is what the most highly regarded winemakers and estates do well: They separate the healthy grapes from the rotten and unripe, and they don't try to make wine from inferior fruit. The wines they make in a bad vintage are often better than the wines made by a poor-quality winemaker in a great vintage. That is why you can enjoy a lifetime of wine and never study a vintage chart. Just follow your growing list of favorite producers.

In Europe, people certainly discuss the great vintages, but they don't quit buying those harvests considered less than great. Many of the top estates, whose wines are in short supply, allocate a small number of bottles to their customers who buy direct, much like the mailing list phenomenon here in the States. If you decline your allocation in a less than stellar vintage, you risk not getting your share in a great year. Many avid collectors will buy every vintage from their favorite domaines and chateaux. The differences between vintages—how the wines taste and when to drink them—provide hours of conversation.

FAMOUS REGIONS

Buying wine based solely on where it comes from can be just as much of a red herring as great vintages. While renowned winegrowing places like Bordeaux and the Napa Valley deserve their great reputations, keep in mind that any accolades these places have earned are based on the best wineries and growers.

If you enjoy all types of wine like me, here's a hypothetical choice for you:

- Tara Bella Winery, Cabernet Sauvignon, from the Russian River Valley
- Ray's Really Good Winery, Cabernet Sauvignon, Napa Valley, from the greatest vintage of the century

In the first instance, many people still don't know a lot about the Russian River Valley, let alone the fact that Cabernet Sauvignon grows there. But Tara Bella and their winemaker have a solid reputation. As for the latter choice, Napa Valley is a trademark of great Cabernet, and we have a super vintage, but who has heard of this winery? As long as you like Cabernet, go for the Tara Bella.

As your list of favorites grows, you may notice certain wine regions dotting your list more often than others. Allow this list of regions to emerge on its own and explore those areas on your holidays. Ask your favorite wineries who they recommend you try. They know each other's work and are often happy to encourage the success of colleagues whom they respect.

Three

THE PRICE OF WINE

Myth: The more it costs, the better it is.
— Frank Prial

USING PRICE AS A SHORTCUT

You're looking at two interesting bottles of Zinfandel in Ray's Really Good Wine Shop. You don't know anything about them other than the price—one sells for $10 and the other is $20. Which is the better wine (which one will give you the most pleasure)? If you choose the more expensive bottle, using price as your only guideline, you're probably spending way more than you need to enjoy wine.

In many of my classes, I'll serve two well-made wines side-by-side, one cheap and one expensive. When I poll the class for their favorite, about half of the participants picks wine *A* while the other half votes for wine *B*.

I see this scenario play out often when tasting sparkling. In class, I will blindfold and serve side-by-side Domaine Carneros' Le Rêve ($40), Roederer Estate's L'Ermitage ($30), and the far more expensive Moët & Chandon Dom Pérignon ($90). Now I've never done this as some sort of rigid statistical experiment.

I just ask for a show of hands, "How many liked number one the best," and so on.

What do they prefer? The voting is often fairly even, about one third of the students each preferring a different wine. Does that mean Moët doesn't make the best wine it could? No, Dom Pérignon is darn good stuff. The big lesson is that we can't use price as a shortcut to figuring out which are the better wines of the world and which we'll enjoy the most. And the great news is that we can buy several bottles of the lesser-known brands for the price of one bottle of Dom!

Determining Price

It doesn't seem to make sense that the Chardonnay you enjoyed last night cost $35 and the one the week before, equally great, was only $15, until you realize that wine prices are not intrinsically tied to quality and pleasure. While prices are not set using a dartboard in the CFO's office, wines are, like other consumer goods, positioned and introduced at a chosen price point that may have little to do with the costs involved in creating them.

Here are some of the factors that go into creating the price of a wine:

1. *Winery Reputation and Story.* Opus One, and its affiliation with the Mondavi and the Rothschild families, is a good example of how reputation and story influence a wine's price. People expect to pay more for the juice that carries this winery's name because the prestige of its founders drives the price beyond what sanity would suggest. It's not deception on the part of the winery to play up its story. It's just that the affection we develop for a winery and its story leads us to pay more than if we were purchasing wine by a more logical formula.

2. *Owner Chutzpah.* If Madonna owned a winery, people would pay for the privilege of visiting. Look at Niebaum-Coppola. They have some stunning wines made by first-

rate winemaking star Scott McLeod. But do you think most people who've seen *The Godfather* know who Scott McLeod is when they visit Francis Ford Coppola's winery? Coppola could fill bottles with Napa dirt and people would buy them.

3. *Celebrity Winemakers.* If a star winemaker, like Helen Turley or Michel Rolland, is consulting on or making the wine, a winery can charge more because the winemaker has a track record for making wines that achieve high scores from the reviewers.

4. *Regional Preference.* The place where the grapes were grown carries financial weight as well. Napa Valley has built a position of quality in people's minds, regardless of the product, and people will pay more for this name.

5. *Availability.* To quote winemaking legend David Ramey, "People want what they can't get." While vineyard designated wines tell consumers precisely where the grapes come from, there's a self-limiting production ceiling tied to the size of the vineyard. A small supply of a sought-after wine equals higher prices.

OTHER EFFECTS

Outside of the winery, critics and wine competitions have an effect on prices. Any score in the 90–100 zone has a wine destined for a price increase. Widely read publications like *Wine Spectator* or Robert Parker's *Wine Advocate* can catapult the sales and fortunes of a winery.

Likewise, a Gold Medal at the San Francisco Chronicle Wine Competition guarantees more sales than a mere Silver or Bronze award. Despite the pedigree of most competitions and esteemed critics, their assessments are only a snapshot in time. The same wine, tasted against a different group of wines on another day, may not fare the same. Nonetheless, the press, the winery, and everyone in the sales channel pick up the score.

Sometimes there is no price increase from the winery. Perhaps the wine is sold-out at the winery, while a great supply of it exists from distributors to retail shops and restaurants. Some will gouge to take advantage of the profit opportunity. Others will raise the price just to slow down the sales, and so maintain the wine on their list of offerings. This may sound bizarre, but part of a retailer and sommelier's strategy is to have a stable inventory of well-regarded products. Highly rated wines build this image and that in turn builds future foot traffic and sales of other wines.

Another reason prices go up on existing wines is the need for price parity on the street. In one fine wine shop where I worked, we regularly raised the prices of collectible wines to keep pace with the auctions. If we didn't, any Tom, Dick, or Harry could have bought a slice of our inventory and sold it on eBay for a tidy profit. It would have been foolish not to keep the prices on par with the current market.

JUDGING A WINE BY ITS BOTTLE

The package that a wine comes in also plays a substantial role in what we're willing to pay. A fancy, heavier-than-average bottle with a slick label commands more money than box wine. After all, box wine just doesn't look as snazzy on the dinner table next to silver candlesticks. A distinctive, but not-too-unusual, bottle shape also sells wine. Think of those Cabernets with the broad shoulders. They may look tastier, yet the wine itself isn't improved by this marketing spin. And we all fall for this, even if our seduction is happening below the conscious level.

Retailers buy into packaging as well. It certainly influenced me in scenarios like the following. A rep is selling two new wines—Chateau Unknown and Chateau Also Unknown. The first wine tastes great and the packaging is sharp. The second wine tastes great and the packaging is lifeless. With a bulging inventory, which one did I buy?—the wine that consumers would pick up to look at when I'm not in the store. I couldn't be in the store all the time, and the inventory had to do some of its own selling.

We are all influenced by appearance and price, and wine experts are not exempt. That is why professional judging is done completely blind. Glasses of wine are already poured, and judges never see the bottles until the competition is complete.

And for yourself at home, you'll only know your true feelings for a wine when you taste it blind. If the bottle says $100, you just expect it to taste better.

Is a $100 Bottle of Wine Better Than a $20 Bottle of Wine?

We started this chapter comparing a $10 and $20 Zinfandel and discussing a number of factors that can build the price of a wine without adding value to it. But what about those triple digit wines? Doesn't a $100 bottle just have to be better than a $20 bottle of wine? Not necessarily. A wine can disappoint at any price, whether $2 or $200. While many great wines are expensive, not all expensive wines are worth their price tag. The price of the $100 wine might be inflated beyond some sort of fair value by factors discussed above, like packaging and scarcity. It may also be of a style or maturity that you wouldn't enjoy. A 1961 Latour might cost a small fortune, but if you prefer the fresh fruit of younger wines, the Latour will surely disappoint you. (For more information, read Brendan Eliason's excellent explanation of the costs of producing a pricey bottle online at www.coffaro.com.)

Yet wines made by the best-reputed producers from fashionable places like Burgundy do cost more and are often worth it. Like the top restaurants, which tend to be expensive, they dazzle you with an experience that McDonald's could never offer. Some of the best meals in my life have, quite frankly, been expensive. At the same time some of the most disappointing meals in my life have been the expensive ones. A pricey meal can disappoint me more than a Big Mac ever could. We just expect more when we spend over $100 per person for dinner, and it's the same with wine.

It's these high expectations that make expensive wine more of a gamble. A friend of mine on a budget has a regular mantra: "I just want to taste _____ [fill in the blank with your most coveted bottle] to see what makes it so special."

That bottle might prove to be a home-run ecstasy or a waste-of-cash disappointment, if the wine doesn't live up to his high expectations. This insight, more often than not, leads me to seek out wines with a better price-to-value relationship.

We know with certainty that a $100 bottle of wine is not five times better than a $20 bottle. You just can't quantify pleasure in this way. The pleasure part is something we make up ourselves, something we perceive when the food, the company, and the wine are in sync. Sometimes that's in a simple stew in the Douro Valley, with a carafe of the house red, shared with those we love. And sometimes it's in a bottle of Krug and a plate of oysters in a Paris Michelin Three Star.

FINDING VALUE

This brings us to the joy and value inherent in drinking the unfashionable. If you like California Chenin Blanc, you can drink your fill and still have money left over to visit the wineries on vacation. Are you a fan of sweet Riesling? You're in luck. Both German and California Rieslings are very undervalued. At one time the great Rieslings of the Mosel in Germany sold for more than the stars of Bordeaux. Relish the opportunity to get a bargain.

If your guests demand a dry white, Sauvignon Blanc is a value the world over. From France's Loire Valley to California's coastal growing regions, this grape and its wines are undervalued. For every Chardonnay over $20, there seems to be an equal number of Sauvignon Blancs under $20.

Like burly reds, packing lots of body and punch? France's Rhône Valley is awash in flavorful, powerful, and affordable red wine. For every California Cabernet over $40, there are at least as many Rhône reds under $40. Enjoy these wines and smile while the rest of America pays too much for Cabernet and Merlot with a posh winery address.

The values are out there if you can resist what is fashionable.

At the opposite end of the retail continuum are the allocated and rare wines. If I could urge just one principle to live by, it's this: Don't buy them. The price-to-value relationship is whacked, and the effort involved to be given the privilege of purchasing them is tantamount to researching your next dissertation.

But if you must, here is the down and dirty. Most of the highly sought-after, limited-production wines are sold directly from the wineries themselves. Get a slot on their mailing lists when you can. Next in line to sell such wine are restaurants, third in the pecking order are non-chain wine shops, and last for a dribble are chain retailers and grocery stores. The odds of obtaining the wines are higher by working from the top of this elevator shaft. You need to develop the relationships and get the timetables of when the wines are released.

If you can't get a reasonable allocation from the winery, don't bother calling the retailers cold. They've heard it all. When you pop in, unknown and unannounced, with your list of *Wine Spectator*'s top-scoring, limited-production wines, your story about your father wanting just one sip of Screaming Eagle before he dies is not going to wash. They'll tell you they don't have any while their coffee cups sit on a box of it in the back room.

To get above the din, you have to develop personal relationships and track what you spend. When your spending goes over $1,000 per year, the staff will probably throw you a few bones. When you start spending over $1,000 a month, they may actually offer a few bones without your having to ask. What a way to buy wine!

Four

RESTAURANT RITUALS

*Can't we just get rid of wine lists? Do we really have
to be reminded every time we go out to a nice restaurant
that we have no idea what we are doing? Why don't
they just give us a trigonometry quiz with the menu?*
— Jerry Seinfeld

Nothing elicits stronger opinions from my students than the subject of trying to enjoy wine in restaurants. Imagine this scene: You're seated with seven of your friends or family, handed a wine list the size of a telephone book, and asked to make a selection. Talk about being on the spot. How much are you going to spend? Who are you going to please? What will you enjoy if you don't know any of the wines? And how can you possibly be ready to order when the waiter returns? You need time to see the menu too!

STRATEGIZING WITH THE WINE LIST

Sometimes there's more pressure: family you don't like, miserly friends who will insist they only drank a glass when the bill arrives, or a really important client that your company is counting on you to schmooze. For your own sanity you've got to minimize the tension around the wine selection, and here are some strategies to help:

- *Advance Reconnaissance.* Visit the restaurant's Web site or phone ahead and ask them to fax a copy of the wine list. This certainly won't work everywhere—Ray's BBQ hasn't put in a computerized cash register, so they certainly haven't posted their list of five wines on the Web. But many restaurants are ready with this info for event planners, who need to map out their wine selections in advance. You can review the wine list at your leisure, ask your wine pals about some of the curiosities, and most importantly, do some price comparison to see where the values lie. Some places ease up on the margins as the price escalates.
- *Find Out What They Like.* At times, this takes detective work, prodding and prying to find out what your guests want when you don't know them well. Two questions that narrow the field immensely: "Dry or sweet?" and "White or Red?" If you don't ask, your polite and non-assertive cousin may end up choking down a few sips of the overpowering, tannic Cabernet that you order. She'll tell you the Cab is good because she doesn't want to insult your taste in wine, especially if you're the perceived expert. And all the while she really wanted a glass of sweet Riesling.
- *Chunk the List.* See what the subsections are and focus only on those wines that are in play for this dinner, looking for your favorite producers, grapes, and the styles of wine your guests desire. Many restaurants have expanded their selections of wine sold by the glass and half bottle, and these subsections provide an opportunity to taste more wines during dinner. Just watch the prices, as some wines sold by the glass don't sport a good price-to-value ratio.
- *Suspect Storage.* Don't order the older bottles if the storage looks suspect. I remember dining in a gorgeous restaurant in the country. The wine was beautifully displayed between the very warm kitchen and the very

warm dining room, and it was obvious that the wine wasn't benefiting from any cool breezes. In these venues, it just isn't worth the gamble to buy wine that has sat in a place of ever-fluctuating temperatures for a long time.

· *Stay on Budget.* If you're entertaining a client, they know what you're spending based on the menu and any knowledge of wine they have. But if you want to keep the talk of price hush-hush, just point to the price points you like on the list, as in, "I'd like something like this," pointing to a price rather than a wine. Best yet is when you can talk about price openly, as in, "We'd like a Chardonnay and Merlot between $20 and $50 each." This directness really narrows the options to a smaller group of choices.

WHAT ABOUT FOOD PAIRING?

Food experts and lovers the world over will gasp when I suggest this next idea, but here it is: Don't be overly concerned with trying to match the food and the wine, and worse, trying to come up with one bottle to do it all. This is a recipe for displeasing someone at the table, including yourself. Paramount is giving people what they like and want. Friends who only like Chardonnay will be much happier if you give them Chardonnay, whether or not they're eating beef tenderloin. You'll be wasting $100 buying the collector Cab to have with their cow. They'll smile politely and tell you what an ace you are with a wine list, but all they really wanted was their Chardonnay.

Likewise if I'm freezing cold, I might want a glass of red wine or if the sun is scorching, I might drink Sauvignon Blanc with my venison bordelaise. It's preference and mood that take priority to please my guests. Pairing food and wine is a passion of many and a fun game to play with friends who truly like all types of wine. Yet the percentage of the population that drinks and enjoys all of the wines you tried in Chapter One is tiny, miniscule, and not to be laughed at. Giving people what they want makes them much happier than exposing them to the wines of the world.

Crowd Pleasing

When you ask your friends what they like, they may insist that it doesn't matter and you should order what you want yourself. When you follow this up by saying, "We're going to get a couple of bottles, so let's get something that you like too," people feel more invited to express their preferences. Get some different wines on the table from the get-go. Often three wines will do the trick for a diverse crowd. Try a dry white, a lightly sweet white, and a dry red and let everybody pass and pour for himself or herself. With several glasses and a pair of hands, people talk and pass wine like it's a cozy Thanksgiving dinner. This breaks the ice as people get into the spirit of sharing the bottles.

To do this well, you have to tell the waiters and waitresses very directly about your plan. You don't want them pouring a half a glass of each wine for every guest. Your guests who only like sweet wine will only drink one of the three glasses poured, and you'll end up with lots of glasses with puddles of unfinished wine. To make this strategy work well, poll your group, find out what they like, order the wine, and explain the wines briefly as you pass the bottles.

Develop a relationship with the waitperson or sommelier, even if only for one night. If the wine list is terribly unfamiliar to you, you'll need their help. You don't want to hear what they like, but as with a helpful assistant in a wine shop, you want someone to understand the styles or types of wines you like and find the winners on the restaurant's wine list.

Traditions Like Nowhere Else

When the sommelier or waitperson brings back your selections and presents the wine to you, the most daunting but necessary ritual unfolds.

Check the label to confirm it's the wine you want. Besides vintage changes, many lists don't fill in all of the details about the wine. You see Robert Mondavi Cabernet Sauvignon, $40 on the list. Is it the Woodbridge bottling at an egregious price, the Reserve bottling at a giveaway price, or one of Mondavi's other Cabs priced in between?

CORK, CORKED, CORKAGE

Has the cork pushed up beyond the top of the bottle, bulging against the foil on top and has the wine leaked? Excess heat expands the volume of wine in a bottle. Though many wines survive this, symptoms of overheating make me nervous about a bottle's condition. Check that you're satisfied before the corkscrew goes into the cork.

When the corkscrew isn't necessary because the wine is already open, my suspicions go wild. There are many chain establishments and bar-oriented restaurants where the staff doesn't need to know much about wine. And neither should they if they're not interested. But training people to open wine at the table doesn't take a lot of effort, and it is definitely preferable to opening the wine at the bar out of the customer's view. I'm not suspecting that they might have poured a different wine into the bottle. My real concern is knowing when the wine was first opened. Was it opened yesterday, sent back by a customer, and now getting a second life? And where is the cork?—In the trash, probably, mixed with lime juice and the staff cigarette butts.

I want that cork. I'm curious about what it looks like, and I want to be able to take any unfinished wine home with me. This is perfectly legal in many places and worth checking into where you live.

Barring the previous unsavory scene of the disappearing cork, the waitress will hand you a cork after opening the bottle. What now? I put it somewhere I can reach it. Later I'll want to feel it and find out if it is synthetic or natural. I'll also look for a brand. In days past, this was another way to check the authenticity of a wine, seeing if the brand on the cork matched the name on the label, though today many corks won't have a brand. The physical appearance of a natural cork seldom correlates with the quality of the wine though much is made of this in the prevailing literature. I've opened countless bottles with ugly, moldy, deteriorating corks and the wines were sound.

If a natural cork is damp, this will indicate that the wine has been laying down, which keeps the cork pliable and puffy, maintaining a better seal over a long time. But if the wine I'm ordering is last year's vintage of Sauvignon Blanc, the position of the bottles during storage is not much of an issue.

What next? Swirl and smell the wine not the cork. Along with poor appearance, a poor smelling cork can be a red herring. A wine going south prematurely, either oxidizing or turning to vinegar, doesn't happen so much anymore. What we're really out to discern is whether or not the wine is *corked*. We say a wine is corked when a substance known as trichloroanisole (TCA) has formed in the cork, transferring into the wine, a smell like wet newspapers and damp cardboard in the basement. Some wines might stink in many other ways that are perfectly acceptable. But the wet cardboard smell originates in the cork, and there's no way to predict it before opening a bottle.

If the wine smells fine, I give the okay and explicit instructions about what I want. I prefer that everyone receive a taste of the wine, a healthy taste rather than a glassful. You can't swirl the wine and enjoy its aromas and bouquets when the glass is too full. I like to give everybody a taste and let the waiter leave. Unless I'm having a very formal business dinner or out with a group of friends whose arms are broken, we can pass and pour the bottles for ourselves. Which leads to another point: Maintain access to the bottle. We've all eaten at pricey places where the service is flawless and your wine is kept on a side table or in a bucket too far away to reach. Don't give up control of that wine. You might want another look at the label or an extra splash while the staff is away.

If I'm suspicious about a wine being tainted with TCA, I'll taste it. A corked wine will usually have its fruit hidden behind a veil of astringency. Now many wines can taste very dry and astringent and be just fine. It's when this astringent taste follows the wet cardboard that I'm concerned. If I'm dead certain of TCA, then I'll say so, letting the server know that the wine is corked. But often there is some doubt. TCA comes in varying intensity and sometimes I'll just say, "I think this is corked, what do you think?" Engage the person waiting on you. Don't start a war. It's not their fault if the wine is off.

They should fetch another bottle of the same, open that, and compare the two wines with you. In most cases, if there is an appreciable difference in the wet newspaper smell, one wine was corked. The restaurant will return it to their supplier and receive full credit for the corked bottle. The frequency of corked wines runs between two and twelve percent of all bottles, depending upon who is paying for the research. In my experience at wine judgings, we'll typically find four to six out of every 100 wines to be corked. This high failure rate is one of the best arguments for alternative closures, especially screwcap tops, which in many cases perform exceptionally well. You can bet we'll see more of them in the future.

If you just don't like the wine, the restaurant really doesn't owe you a different bottle. In the restaurants where I have worked, we often heard people say a wine was bad if it was tannic and tough as old boots. The wine needed time to evolve, but it wasn't bad. When you don't like the wine, you really have to weigh the effect of pouting about something you're not happy with versus bucking up and sticking to your choice. I tend to err on the side of being agreeable. I've even drunk wines that I knew were a little corked when I knew that there was too much of a language barrier to get my point across.

Another variation on the word *cork* is *corkage*, which is a different subject entirely. If you want to bring your own wine to a restaurant, you can pay the corkage, or the fee a restaurant charges to open and serve this wine for you. Fees range from reasonable to absurdly high.

You might go this route if you want to share a sentimental bottle or to save money. Both are good reasons. But if you do bring your own bottle, bear in mind that this can result in hostile feelings from the wait staff.

Also:

- Most restaurants won't accept you bringing a wine they already sell on their list, and you can't blame them. Call ahead to check on your bottle and what it will cost you in corkage.
- The wait staff whose tips depend on building a higher rather than lower check average might be alienated by your strategy, precipitating a drop in service and sometimes outright hostility. To mitigate this result, share the wine with the staff and factor its value into the tip. The service level may actually go up.

Five

SERVING WINE AT HOME

*Dinner would have been splendid... if the wine had been as
cold as the soup, the beef as rare as the service, the brandy
as old as the fish, and the maid as willing as the Duchess.*
— Winston Churchill

When your guests arrive for your next dinner party, offer
them something different, like an aperitif. In Europe there
seems more of a tradition of drinking an aperitif before dinner.
If your guests are adventurous and enjoy all styles of wine, offer
them a Kir. You can dress up a glass of cheap, dry, white plonk
with a smidgin of crème de cassis, creating a visually appealing,
lightly purple, cold glass of wine with a hint of sweetness. People
drink this around the world, and you can make it as sweet or
dry as you like just by varying the amount of cassis. Splurge on
a good bottle of cassis from France for around $20. The cheap
brands just don't have the fruit concentration, and you use so
little with each glass of wine, a bottle will last for a year in your
refrigerator. Similarly, you can dress up a budget, dry, sparkling
wine by using your cassis to create a Kir Royale.

Another aperitif, sweet vermouth, is an aromatic wine,
which is sweet and bitter at the same time. For me, it's the best

bet to refresh a palate that has endured a day of coffee, tea, or cola. In the summer it's great served cold over ice with a slice of citrus. You can buy great Italian (Cinzano and Martini & Rossi) or French (Noilly Prat) vermouth for less than $10 a bottle and enjoy a glass periodically. It stays fresh in the fridge, protected by its higher alcohol level.

On the dry end of the spectrum, Fino Sherry, from a top producer like Lustau, is also a very affordable and equally refreshing aperitif. Yet, unlike sweet vermouth, this wine demands a love of the driest of the dry wines. Like very dry Champagne or an acidic Sauvignon Blanc, Fino Sherry feels incredibly lean and crisp. With fried anchovies and salty olives there may be no better match, especially if you're dining in the summer heat of southern Spain.

TOOLS

There is a vast array of wine openers and many of the most modern operate on a principle of leverage, just like an old-fashioned waiter's corkscrew. A waiter's corkscrew works so well compared to a T-shaped model because there is a lever assisting you. The high-tech models make this even easier, though they still require some effort and can be troublesome with wax capsules and synthetic corks.

The gargantuan models that you see mounted on bar tops can be super easy to use, but are a bit like using a sledgehammer on a thumbtack when you need to open an old bottle. They're so powerful that they often push a cork right in. For old wines it's often best to use an Ah-So, the two pronged gadget that slips down the sides of the cork rather than going into it.

More important than the particular choice or brand of opener is having more than one on hand. And if you keep an extra corkscrew in your glove compartment, you'll prove the hero at a picnic someday when the host forgets to pack one.

Glassware

Wineglasses are important. There's something missing in the experience of drinking wine from a coffee mug. Wine is not just about the flavors; it's also a tactile experience—from the texture of the wine on your tongue to the feel of the glass in your hand. Wine is a visual experience as well, and watching the bubbles stream up a glass of sparkling can be far more stress-reducing than watching the television.

You can spend a fortune on wineglasses to enhance this experience, but it isn't necessary. Buy what's comfortable for your budget because pricey glasses break as easily as cheap ones, if not more so.

More important is the shape of the glass. A glass that tapers inward at the top (the opening is smaller than the bowl at the bottom) helps to concentrate the scent of a wine, which is a great part of its pleasure. Also, it saves on dry cleaning, as you're less likely to spill your wine when you swirl it.

A stem is nice, especially in the summer when you might want your Riesling to stay cold at lunch, not warmed up by the full grip of your paws. But stems aren't necessary and don't let anyone tell you otherwise. I recall dining in a restaurant where the wine glasses were microscopic and impossible to swirl without the wine flying out. I handled my water glass, appreciating how tall and big it was and the light bulb went off. I asked for an empty one and transferred my wine. No stem and a better experience.

Big is good in glassware. Again, it's easier to swirl the wine without it leaping out of the glass. For the same reason, a large glass is more practical when you're walking in the garden with your wine. Buy them by the box or case, so they're easy to store and pack for a trip in the country. This also saves the chore of dusting glasses that have been out on display in a hanging rack above the kitchen counter. It's practical as well if you're invited to a group winetasting at someone's home or a class where everyone brings his or her own glasses. Just dry your glasses thoroughly before storing them. They can, however, pick up the smell of the box so you might have to wash them anyway before the next use. If you have the room, the ideal storage seems to be in a clean cupboard, on a mesh of some type, that allows air to flow in the glass.

How many different sizes and shapes do you need? Two is a good place to start: one flute or tulip shape for sparkling and one large all-purpose wineglass for the wines without bubbles. If you have room for more, pick up a set of smaller wineglasses, not for your white wines, but just to suit your mood. Sometimes you just feel like handling a smaller glass, like those days when you want to drink your beer out of the can rather than a large pint glass.

And if you're tired of washing so many glasses after dinner, just use one or two per guest. When you taste lots of different wines on the same evening, sequence your wines from white to red and light to heavy and you won't need to rinse with water in between. About the only time I rinse with water is when we go from tasting a red wine back to white, as when we finish a meal with a white dessert wine. Sometimes at extensive tastings, we'll rinse with just a smidgin of the next wine we're going to taste. It seems a waste but nothing rinses wine from a glass like another wine.

What else is important about the glass? It's easier to see the wine in smooth crystal as opposed to cut glass with lots of facets. For the same reason, clear glass is a priority choice over any color, even in the base or stem. You can pick up some very functional glassware (costing between $3 and $5 each) and you will be prepared for any great wine that your guests bring. Should you buy the pricey crystal in a complex array of shapes and sizes? While it has been demonstrated that the shape of a glass influences the flavor of wine, you could drive yourself crazy matching wine and glasses, and I wouldn't advise buying more than your partner will tolerate. As for how much you spend, it depends on how many you can afford to break, because they will.

THE HOT POINTS ON SERVING TEMPERATURE

As a wine gets cooler, its acidity and tannin are accentuated, which is why a cold dry red wine doesn't taste so great. But neither is a warm one. A room-temperature Cabernet, when the summer heat is over 90 degrees, is not pleasant. This is why the French, winemakers included, are not averse to putting their reds in an ice bucket for ten or fifteen minutes to take the edge off when the temperature is scorching. And many fruity reds are traditionally served a little cooler, as are some sweet reds and tawny ports for dessert.

On the other hand, if we chill the heck out of a white wine, we certainly won't taste as much of it, like ice-cold beer versus cool beer. Now maybe ice cold is good when the wine tastes like crap. You don't want to taste too much of it. But if it's yummy, you might want to drink it a little warmer than usual. Take it out of the fridge and let it sit on the table or hold the bulb of the glass in the palm of your hand. All this aside, personal preference rules over any notion of proper serving temperature.

Out of time and need cold wine? We've all stuck a bottle in the freezer before dinner. It's not criminal as some would suggest and not much different from the waiter plunking the Chardonnay you ordered directly from its case into an ice bucket beside your table. Just don't forget about the wine while it's out of sight in the freezer. Alternatively, you can fill an ice bucket or pot with cold water, ice, and salt for a quick chill—a faster method than ice alone.

DECANTERS

When it comes to these crystal vessels, you can spend a fortune. Artsy designs alone won't make the wine taste better, but they do look good on the table. Physically decanting a wine can enhance flavor, but it depends upon the age of the wine. A young, tough-as-shoe-leather Petite Sirah might benefit from exposure to air, which allows flavors to surface and makes the wine more approachable. In contrast, older wines are very fragile and a long session of breathing might just give away the tender flavors and smells to the atmosphere. However, decanting an old wine will allow you to separate the wine from the sediment that has deposited in the bottle.

To decant a young wine, pour the wine into a decanter once or twice and let it sit open. How far in advance to do this is the unknown. More time, a few hours or a day, may help. You really have to have tasted the wine recently or talked to someone who has. Nobody can say with certainty the best amount of time to let wine breathe. It's just educated guessing, based on experience with the particular wine in question. What all of us can agree on is the fact that not much breathing occurs by pulling a cork and setting the bottle on the table.

Before decanting an older wine, stand the bottle up for a day or two to allow the loosest sediment to fall to the bottom. There's nothing wrong with the sediment; it's just not pleasant ingesting the little gritty bits. When you're ready to drink, open the wine, position the decanter on a counter next to a burning candle or upturned flashlight and turn the bottle over gradually toward the decanter, allowing the neck to rest over the light. Pour the wine easily, without any glugging, and when the sediment starts to appear in the neck, stop. You can filter this last ounce or so with an unbleached coffee filter later or just give it to the angels.

As you see from this discussion, wine changes with its exposure to air. Just notice how a wine changes and evolves while swirling it in a glass. That half-empty bottle of monster Zinfandel may taste better on the second night, just as it would have if we had decanted it a day ahead of drinking it. Lots of other wines, however, might be toast by tomorrow if we don't do something to mitigate the influence of oxygen.

Leftovers

One easy approach to managing your leftovers is to save some empty half bottles and pour your remainders into these. Some people like to use the devices that pull air from a half-empty bottle, while others prefer to spray inert gas in the bottle to replace the oxygen. Another strategy is to blend all of your leftover wines of the same color to make as many full bottles as possible. This preserves the leftovers effectively and you create your own proprietary blends. All of these methods have their supporters and detractors. I think you have to experiment for yourself and see what suits you best. Taking some minimal action in this area allows you to enjoy a few different wines every evening rather than opening just one bottle at a time.

In any case, put your leftovers in the fridge and pull out the reds when you return from work the next evening. Then they'll warm up before dinner and be ready to drink.

Six

BEYOND FOOD
AND WINE PAIRING

I cook with wine, sometimes I even add it to the food.
— W.C. Fields

HOSPITALITY

The doorbell rings and your guests enter knowing they're in store for another great evening. Why do they love to come to your home? Is it your collection of first-growth Bordeaux, your penchant for serving the latest in wine-drinking trends, or the fact that you lecture them on the vintages and vineyards of the wines you serve? Likely none of these answers hits the mark. It's hospitality that makes the difference. If people of diverse backgrounds enjoy themselves and feel welcomed into your home, they'll return eagerly, regardless of your wine knowledge.

One of the tips I learned early in the restaurant business was to let the guests leave feeling they were denied nothing. We think nothing of brewing a pot of tea for one friend out of six at the table that doesn't share our love of coffee, but how often do we try to make one choice of wine please everyone. If you're not serving aperitifs, open the bottles for dinner, more than one, before or as your guests arrive. Let them see that the choices are plentiful by opening something dry and something sweet.

How often I've heard people say, "Let's open this one and see how it goes." Ultimately it goes poorly for a polite friend who won't say a word about their preference for dry over sweet or vice versa. Likewise when we ask our guests what they would like to drink, they often remark that whatever you have open is fine. Many feel it's an imposition upon your hospitality to have a bottle opened especially for them, saying politely, "Don't open that just for me." If the choices are already open, this hurdle is handled.

This also gives your adventurous guests a chance to try more than one wine. And if you serve the same wines at dinner, they'll have a preview of what they'll enjoy and hate before they're seated.

Serving many different wines doesn't mean getting our friends plowed. They have to be able to drive home safely if taking to the road after dinner, and today we're blessed with some great beverages sans alcohol. Navarro Vineyards in California's Anderson Valley is one example of a winery bottling some first-rate grape juice. Sonoma Sparkler, also from California, is a refreshing 100 percent sparkling juice with Champagne qualities and a light, crisp taste. A glass or two of these before dinner could be just what the designated driver needs to moderate their wine intake over the course of an evening. The other great moderator is water—having plenty available expands the choices for your guests and keeps them hydrated.

Wine and food pairing is great fun and makes for lively discussions when your friends are game and open to all kinds of wine. But if Mom only likes White Zinfandel, let her be and don't try to educate her on the principles of food and wine pairing.

Yin and Yang of Food and Wine

This brings us to the yin and yang of food and wine pairing and three simple approaches to think about when putting your menu together.

1. *Reflective Properties.* In the arena of reflecting tastes, rich food like a chicken breast with cream sauce would pair nicely with a rich and buttery Chardonnay. A sweet dessert like crème caramel would be reflected by a very sweet white dessert wine like Sauternes. A highly acidic dish like spaghetti with a marinara sauce shines when paired with a highly acidic wine like Barbera from Italy's Piedmont. The Barbera also benefits by tasting a bit softer when paired with such a dish; just as a piece of goat cheese takes off the acidic edge of a zippy Sauvignon Blanc from Sancerre in France's Loire Valley. A wine that is low in acid will taste correspondingly flat when up against the zip of a highly acidic dish.

   · Rich Food Reflects Rich Wine
   · Acidic Food Reflects Acidic Wine

2. *Counterpoint.* From this point of view, a foil to the richness rather than a reflection of it would enhance the chicken breast and cream sauce. An acidic and concentrated Pinot Grigio from the northeast of Italy, would do the job of cutting through the fatty, rich dish. Likewise, a Russian River Pinot Noir, with an acidic backbone, would provide the counterpoint to a grilled salmon and white butter sauce.

   · Rich Food Sliced by Acidic Wine

3. *Complete the Palate.* Enhance the dining experience by adding to the palate a different flavor or sensation with the wine. Think about lemonade and its zest of acidity that is balanced by the sweetness of sugar, making a more complete and enjoyable range of flavors. Or, prosciutto

and melon—on its own, there is a great balance of fruity sweetness and a salty tang. Some combinations of food do this dance so well they seem to make the choice of wine irrelevant. Nevertheless, a salty piece of ham tastes even better with a lightly sweet Riesling. A sweet Chenin Blanc cools the heat of a spicy Thai shrimp dish. Salty potato chips shine with dry Champagne.

·   Salty Food   +   Sweet Wine
·   Salty Food   +   Acidic Wine
·   Spicy Food   +   Sweet Wine

All three of these approaches seek a balance and harmony between the food and the wine. There are so many workable combinations that you needn't chase the elusive dream of creating the perfect match of wine and food. And honestly, it's more likely than not that your choice of wine and food will work well together. I've had so many enjoyable meals with whatever wine I was in the mood for.

Many of the specific dictums about wine and food pairing break down because a particular wine can have so many different styles. For instance some Cabernets are very tough and tannic and others are light and fruity. It's almost impossible to say without exception that Cabernet Sauvignon goes well with ____ ____ (You fill in the blank). Yes, as you study wine, you start to see generalities emerge about the different wine grapes. But you really can't be sure how a specific wine will taste until you open a bottle or talk to someone who recently has. Likewise, you won't know how your beurre blanc is going to taste until you've made it. Sometimes mine is a little more acidic, sometimes less.

A Few Pitfalls

What's easier to say with certainty is that there are a few pitfalls to avoid in the realm of food and wine pairing, and it's quicker to say what not to do than the other way around.

1. A green salad with a classic French or Italian vinaigrette is tough to pair with wine because of the acidity of the dressing and the amount of water in some lettuces. A soft, plush Chardonnay will get wiped out, while a highly acidic, dry sparkling wine or a zippy Sauvignon Blanc are better candidates. In my days working in a traditional French restaurant, we often took a different tack, advising guests to take a break from the wine for one course. Alcohol is dehydrating, and if you're reading this book, you're unlikely to be drinking water with your next lobster. Water with your salad provides some balance in your menu and for your liver.

   If you're having salad as a main course and aren't giving up wine, Sonoma chef Mary Evely suggests making your vinaigrette with a 4:1 ratio of oil to vinegar, to ensure that the dressing won't be overly acidic.

2. Spicy food is hard on wine and the burning fire can multiply exponentially with a dry, tannic, or high-alcohol wine. Some folks really enjoy acidic white wines, like Sauvignon Blanc, with spicy seafood. For me, though, the best bet is to pair lightly sweet white wines with your next curried prawns or sushi, especially if you're one to pile on the wasabi. If you're a die-hard red wine drinker, however, we have found some workable pairings with spicy cuisine. Best bets are California Zinfandel, Australian Grenache, and Shiraz from either country, where the wine is ripe and jammy, almost a sweet expression of fruit, while at the same time, low in tannin and not burning with the taste of alcohol. These wines can really complement spicy meat dishes.

3. Save your older, trophy bottles for simply prepared dishes that won't overwhelm the wine. If, however, your young and tannic, prized Cabernet is beckoning to be opened, serve it with some heavier, protein-rich food like a steak or

English Cheddar. These foods will soften the hard edges of an infant bottle.

4. Beware of dry wine with sweet food. When serving a wine with dessert, it is essential to the marriage that the wine be at least as sweet as the dessert, if not more so. And many desserts are hugely sweet.

The one exception to this last idea is the phenomenon of chocolate and dry red wine. While many enjoy their after-dinner chocolate with sweet red wines like Port or Banyuls from the south of France, a contrary movement has swept California's tasting rooms: namely, chocolate, especially bittersweet, with Cabernet Sauvignon or Zinfandel. Food experts disagree about the combination, while others lap it up.

Seven

GIVING
THE GIFT OF WINE

*Drawing a cork is like attendance at a concert or at a play
that one knows well, when there is all the uncertainty of no
two performances ever being quite the same. That is why the
French say, 'There are no good wines, only good bottles.'*
— Gerald Asher, On Wine

After your boss has savored the last sip of the Dom Pérignon
you gave her for Christmas, what will she think of you and
your generosity?

RECONNAISSANCE MISSION

While selecting a gift can cause bad dreams, giving wine to
colleagues and clients can cause nightmares. And the stakes are
raised when you spend a huge sum of money and don't even
know if she likes Champagne. As with other gifts, a thoughtful
wine present takes some reconnaissance, watching for clues,
and asking subtle questions about the recipient's preferences.
It's easy to work in the subject if you talk with them about food.
Wine follows quite naturally, as in, "What kind of wine did you

have with that scrumptious lobster custard?" In this context you can swing the subject toward their favorite wines.

When reconnaissance fails, however, you can hedge your bets with some of the following strategies.

To begin, what wine might she enjoy most, white or red? While many people drink either, some quite decidedly prefer one or the other. If you don't know the answer, the odds are safer with white. It's not because there are more white wine drinkers than red. It's because red wine drinkers can almost always lighten to white, yet many white wine drinkers cannot tolerate the heavier weight of red wine. If you have a suspicion that they drink both, a red is almost always more highly valued. Just look at today's prices for red and white wines. Red is in vogue.

The broad range of whites available leads us to the next question: does she prefer sweet or dry wine? If she seldom drinks wine, sweet is a safer bet.

Sweetness is soothing for a die-hard fan of Coke and 7 UP and a sweet Riesling or Gewürztraminer will hit closer to the mark than any dry Sauvignon Blanc or Merlot. The most experienced wine drinkers also adore sweet wine and cherish it as a gift.

Dry wine is the hedge bet for people who drink wine everyday. Such a person undoubtedly likes dry wine and dry wine has the added advantage of a swankier image among the *nouveau cognoscenti* of wine drinking. Such a person might think you committed a faux pas if you gave them a sweet wine. These snobs often wander in a pretentious phase for a few years, thinking that only dry wine is a sophisticated beverage. Later down the wine-drinking road, they'll come to appreciate Eiswein and Tawny Port (See the Dry vs. Sweet section in Chapter 10).

THE CHECKUP

Watch what you spend on the gift of wine because your recipient might check up on you. I don't know how many times it happened when I worked in retail that someone would come in with a question about the price of a wine. I'd engage them in conversation about the wine, and, inevitably, they would look at the floor, smile a bit like a guilty kid, and confess that they didn't actually want to buy any. They were given a bottle and wondered what it might be worth.

You can kind of understand this happening. People have a sense of what an Hermès scarf or a pair of Levi's costs, but not so with wine. So we might hope that the recipient just wants to get a sense of whether to save this bottle for a special occasion or savor it with next week's pizza.

The flipside of this scenario is buying a very expensive, obscure wine that collectors would die for and your recipient has no idea of the price, the story, and the difficulty it took to come by. If you give such a bottle to a client and really want them to know how special it is, you've wasted your money. You can't come out and say, "Hey, I drove all over town just to find this $100 bottle for you!"

Both sides of this rocky hard place demand a recognizable purchase. Something that he or she looks at and says, "Wow, that was really special of you to get this for me."

Now I'm not advocating throwing money away on wine. For me, cheap or pricey, it's far more interesting to purchase a wine I've never tasted from a producer I have yet to study. Ultimately I want value. I want to learn more about and to taste wines that are a good value for the money.

But giving wine as a gift is a different animal with its own peculiar traps. Hedge your bets on the red/white and sweet/dry questions and buy something people will understand, appreciate, and rave about.

Eight

CHAMPAGNE

I like Champagne because it tastes as though my foot's asleep.
—Art Buchwald

WHAT'S IN A NAME?

What's in a name anyway? When the name is Champagne, it's charged with energy, from the fizz of its bubbles to the battles over what Champagne means.

Most people speak of any sparkling wine as Champagne. It's the way people speak, and I cringe when wine geeks tell people that they're wrong for using the word so liberally. The philosopher Wittgenstein argued that the meaning of words really comes down to their usage. In other words, the way people use a word or expression is what creates its meaning. And the reality is that people call any wine with fizz *Champagne*. Even our own Alcohol and Tobacco Tax and Trade Bureau in Washington, D.C., which regulates U.S. wine label laws, allows the use of the word Champagne on domestically produced bottles of bubbly. Watch future WTO rulings on this.

French Champagne

Yet the French use the word *Champagne* in a more restrictive way based on some good historical reasons. In France, the place where the grapes are grown to create a wine is of paramount importance. So much so that the prevailing view in France is that the same variety of grapes grown in different locations— even across the road—will produce different tasting wines. This concept of *terroir*—that everything about a vineyard, from the angle of the hillside to the direction it faces to the soil beneath it and the climate around it, will create a unique wine—is a widely held view among winegrowers in and outside of France.

These subtleties of farming provide hours of conversation for wine aficionados all over the world. More compelling to the growers in the southern Rhône was the need to identify their grapes and wine to the larger wine-drinking public. In a previous era, they developed and pushed for a system of controlled place names to further distinguish their wines and grapes from those of Burgundy and Bordeaux. They needed to establish a brand identity, if you will, to get a larger slice of the pie. Their goal was achieved, and today a system of controlled place names is the law of the land in France, so that if a wine says Châteauneuf-du-Pape on the label, it comes from Châteauneuf-du-Pape; if a cheese is labeled Roquefort, it is aged in the caves of Roquefort-sur-Soulzon.

The geeks truncate this story and tell their friends that it's *improper* to call sparkling wine Champagne unless it comes from a demarcated wine region in France named Champagne. The geeks are right: In France, one would not call a sparkling wine "Champagne" if made outside of the demarcated region of Champagne. And many experts would agree. Yet, I can't be bothered to join them in making nine out of ten people wrong when they ask for a glass of Champagne at their favorite bar or restaurant. It's just too abrasive.

Yes, Champagne is an important place in France, but its production methods have also become a worldwide standard, and many producers have adopted the name Champagne or derivatives of that, like *méthode champenoise* or *méthode traditionnelle* to signal that they too have been making bubbly with an eye toward quality.

A Sparkling Value

It's these alternative sparklers that provide us with the greatest value for the money. Sparkling is made throughout France, from Chenin Blanc in the Loire Valley to Pinot Blanc in Alsace. The names of these wines are too numerous to mention, but they are notable for the absence of the word Champagne on their labels. Along with the brand names of the wineries that made them, you'll often see references to the place where the grapes were grown, like Limoux, and a word to indicate bubbles, like *Crémant*.

Spain provides us with a great supply of affordable bubbly, and in Italy, there are great sparklers produced in Franciacorta near Milan, which rival France's treasured Champagne. Further east, in the Veneto, we find the fruity Prosecco made in varying degrees of sweetness from the grape of the same name.

Selecting a sparkler that fits your mood on the following dry-to-sweet scale is far more important than choosing between France, a region within France, or another country.

LABEL	SWEETNESS	POPULAR BRAND
NATURAL OR EXTRA BRUT	*Little to no residual sugar —Very Dry*	*Korbel Laurent-Perrier*
BRUT	*Small amounts of residual sugar —Very Dry*	*Roederer Estate, Mumm Cuvée Napa, Bollinger*
EXTRA DRY	*Moderate residual sugar —Medium Dry*	*Korbel Ruggeri, Chandon Riche*

LABEL	SWEETNESS	POPULAR BRAND
DEMI-SEC	*Noticeable residual sugar —Lightly Sweet*	*Veuve Clicquot, Schramsberg*
SPUMANTE MOSCATO D'ASTI OR ASTI	*Pronounced residual sugar —Quite Sweet*	*Ballatore, Ceretto, Martini & Rossi*

There are a few super-dry sparklings that sport words like *natural* or *brut nature* on the label. These have little or no sweetness at all. Wines labeled *brut* often have some measure of sweetness yet most don't come across as such because much of the quality sparkling in the world is chock-full of acidity. A hint of residual sugar rounds out the flavor, in essence, easing the bracing quality of the acidity and filling out the palate. So while a wine labeled *brut* may have some sugar in it, we may never notice it. And a very ripe *brut nature* can taste less austere than a wine labeled *brut*. Because of the range of acidity, sweetness, and the interplay of the two, the feeling of sweetness varies a bunch.

A touch sweeter are wines labeled *extra dry*. Eons ago, when most bubbly was sweet, this term denoted a not-so-sweet wine. Wines in this category can make a great aperitif, their light sweetness making an easy entry into dinner. They're also easier on the palate at brunch, just as a little sugar helps coffee go down first thing in the morning.

Another notch higher in sweetness is a tiny number of wines labeled *demi-sec*. These wines pair nicely with savory foods just like those lightly sweet Rieslings and Chenin Blancs. Even with the extra sweetness, these wines still aren't sweet enough to pair well with dessert.

My absolute favorites on the sweetest side of the spectrum are the wines of Piedmont in Italy's northwest and their imitators in the New World. Of all the wines poured in my classes, none elicits a bigger "wow!" than Moscato d'Asti. Most people go bananas over this adult Kool-Aid®. Only a handful of people don't, and most of them are biased by the notion that sweet sparkling is cheap and shoddy.

On a hot summer evening, nothing is better with fresh berries than Moscato d'Asti, made from the white Muscat grape. The low alcohol of these wines, about 5 percent, is easier to digest when the weather is heavy and there's sweat on your brow.

A restaurant professional once confessed, "I have to admit, I like this!" after tasting another of these Piedmont-style gems, this time a sparkling red Freisa from Bonny Doon in California. How did we ever get so far from enjoying sweet wine that we have to talk about it in the cautious tones of a therapy session?

THE OTHER SPARKLING REVELATION

My students often vote for the top California sparklers when tasted blind, side-by-side, against the big guns of France. Domaine Carneros' Le Rêve versus Moët's Dom Pérignon? Le Rêve wins or ties the legend of Champagne. One of my favorites on the dry end of the sparkling spectrum, Roederer Estate's L'Ermitage from Mendocino County's Anderson Valley, often takes the prize when up against Clicquot's La Grande Dame. I could be accused of being a cheerleader for the wine country in which I live, but I'm no parochial stooge. I just revel in seeing a $40 bottle upstage a $100 bottle in a blind tasting.

How is it that the Californians can compete against the great names of Champagne? For all of the emphasis on Champagne as a region that grows great grapes for making sparkling wine, it must be acknowledged that few types of wine absorb as much of a winemaker's imprint as sparkling. With a great winemaker, modern equipment, a no-skimping-on-quality attitude, and good grapes, great sparkling can be made in far more places on the planet than the Champagne marketers would have us believe.

The last revelation is that vintage sparkling is not by definition better than non-vintage wine. To battle the perceived downscale image of non-vintage wine, some producers are opting to call their non-vintage bottlings, *multivintage*. I can't blame them for the marketing spin: masterful blending of multiple vintages, as done by Krug and Laurent-Perrier, can produce wines of immense complexity and deliciousness.

THE NUTS AND BOLTS OF BUBBLY

While a pop sounds great, it's a rushing exit of pressure. So let it pop if you want the audible effect, but a gentle opening and a whisper of gas preserves more of the bubbles that make Champagne so special.

Not many people are injured, but you don't want to risk someone's future by pointing a bottle at them during the opening. Hold the bottle at a 45-degree angle to minimize the foaming, and keep a good grip on the cork.

People love cold bubbly and you can err on the side of frigidness with this wine. A good chill also keeps the bubbles tighter, smaller, and longer lasting. If the occasion is impromptu, dunk the bottle in a bath of ice and cold water, and for a super rapid chill, dump a healthy quantity of salt in the bucket.

Invest in a Champagne stopper for less than $5 and you can preserve your bubbly for later in the week. Sometimes a few glasses are just enough and you create another occasion on a successive day. Just make sure to buy a stopper with a nub—a sort of nipple—which fits into the bottle. Though most of these gadgets lock, the flat stoppers can slide off if your bottle is sloshing around in a cooler.

CHAMPAGNE AND FOOD

- With sashimi and sushi, yes!
- Champagne marries well with a salty cheese like Parmesan.
- Champagne can stand up to a vinaigrette salad dressing better than most wines because of its formidable acidity.

- The high acidity of sparkling also means that it cuts through the oily weight of gravlax.
- Champagne with your wedding cake can be disastrous. It's almost impossible to find a Champagne sweet enough to work. Best to try an Asti if you insist on sparkling.
- Champagne brunch? If you're planning on extra helpings of the shrimp cocktail and freshly shucked oysters at the seafood buffet, by all means indulge. If you fancy an omelet, stick with beer; it's my favorite for a "breakfast of champions."
- Fried, crunchy foods are great with sparkling. It took me years to see the light on the pairing of potato chips and Champagne. Don't waste as much time as I did. Penny Gadd-Coster at J recommends a little dollop of crème fraîche and caviar on the chips.
- Steve Pitcher recommends popcorn, too.
- The sweet sparklings like Asti and Moscato d'Asti are delicious with fresh berries and ice cream.
- There's such a mesmerizing quality to a tall flute of Champagne that I often take it solo with a comfortable chair outdoors.

Lastly, sparkling wine isn't just for special occasions and this wine has a way of making any occasion feel special. People feel honored when you open a bottle of bubbly in a way that you just can't duplicate with a cold Budweiser.

Nine

AGING GRACEFULLY

Wine improves with age. The older I get, the better I like it.
— Anonymous

A bottle of wine takes on mythic status as it ages. We wait for it to get better, often expecting a glorious experience proportional to the number of years it has rested in our care.

Over time, the whites change in color from greens and yellows to brown, and the reds evolve from purple and red to orange and brown. The tannins and acidity soften and the fruit evolves, changing from fresh to dry, like the change from fresh grapes to raisins and fresh plums to prunes. The color, fruit flavors, and structure of sparkling wine change in the same way and the prized feature, the bubbles, diminish.

Complexity is a pretty foggy term, said to increase as a wine ages. It's a way of saying that more flavors form as the components of the wine marry. It's like that soup your mother made when you were little—it always tasted better the second day. But this gradual improvement doesn't last forever, and after some time, that soup will taste past its prime. Likewise with wine, a day will come when the bottle is no longer a pleasure to drink, and there's no way to precisely predict when this will be.

It's really only by tasting a wine periodically that we know how it is evolving. Some wines have a very short straight, downhill curve, like Moscato d'Asti and Beaujolais Nouveau, which we prize for their fresh, fruity character. Most New World Sauvignon Blanc and Pinot Gris are so delicious when young that I never wait to see how they might age. You can visualize wines of this type on a very steep curve.

Other wines need time to become pleasurable, like a tightly wound, tannic Cabernet Sauvignon. Its enjoyment can be pictured on a much softer curve.

The longer the potential life of a wine, the longer will be its peak of performance. Yet even with a large window of pleasure, there are countless bottles all over the world that would have been enjoyed more if they were opened sooner rather than later. As always, personal and cultural preferences should win out over any expert's determination of the best time to drink a particular wine. Some people love the taste of older wine, while others just shrug and ask what all the fuss is about. And frankly, a passion for older wine is an acquired taste, like coffee or dark beer. No one I know has exited the womb looking for a cup of espresso.

What we can be sure of is this: If the wine in question is on many collectors' want list, its value will increase over time. It's valuable because there are fewer bottles available to the world of collectors, not because the wine is getting magically better each year—it could be past its peak. While drinking a bottle of 1961 Latour can be a delicious experience, its value is really amplified by the fact that there are far fewer bottles of this wine available than there were in 1965.

STORING YOUR PRECIOUS WINE TREASURES

For folks in a small living space, offsite rental storage may be the only answer. You get temperature-controlled safety, but for a price. And besides the money, you lose easy access.

A dusty wine cellar is much more romantic than a storage locker, but few of us have cellars and a closet in the right spot may serve well enough. I've seen wine stored quite successfully in temperatures ranging from a fairly constant 50 degrees to a fairly constant 70 degrees. Just remember that higher temperatures push the evolution of the wine along more quickly and too high a temperature, especially above 90 degrees, can introduce cooked flavors that may not be to your liking. Older wines purchased directly from a winery often taste much younger than those that have languished on a retail shelf for years. It's not just the height of the temperature that we must watch, but the variance as well. I would take a room that was forever at 70 degrees over one that bobbed up and down between 45 and 75.

You can purchase a maximum/minimum thermometer used by gardeners to get a gauge on your storage space. Stick it in all of your closets for a few weeks to see which one stays the most constantly cool. Some people add air conditioning and insulation to their cubbyhole and realize good success in storing their wine.

Lay the bottles on their sides or upside down to keep the corks moist. This keeps them plump and more effective at keeping air out of the bottles, preventing premature oxidation. I like to keep my bottles in racks on their sides, so it's easier to see the labels. The humidity of a cellar is more wine friendly, but with the corks sufficiently wet with wine, you needn't trouble over maintaining a swamp-like environment.

If your home is devoid of a suitable space for storing your wine, you can also purchase a freestanding wine refrigerator, which works at higher temperatures than the fridge where you store your food. A cheap but effective alternative is to store your wine in an old fridge or freezer that you don't turn on. It's like a giant insulated box.

Whether you opt for a cellar, closet, or cabinet, all of these alternatives keep your wine out of the sun and house lights, further preserving your treasures. They also keep your bottles out of view of guests who might want to try them. Viewing your wine collection is part of the pleasure of having it, and you can always share a peek with your like-minded friends. Just bear in mind that it will bore some of your friends to tears.

Creating a wine storage area, however modest, also helps keep you from drinking the treasures you want to keep. For every person the number of bottles is different, but for me it took amassing ten cases to be able to let the giants lie. It's too easy to open a wine you know would benefit from aging when the alternatives at hand are few. If you only have a few bottles in the house, the odds are that one night soon, you'll open that 2000 Taylor Vintage Port because it was handy and you needed something to drink with the chocolate decadence your friend popped in with. If you had twenty other bottles of Port, however, you might let that baby of a Taylor sleep quietly.

So when should you drink your rare gems that are supposed to improve over time? If you buy them in large enough quantities, you can taste a bottle here and there over time. Call the producer and get a ballpark idea of when the wine might be optimal, especially if someone on the staff has tried your vintage recently. Often the wine publications review older vintages and this can provide some guidance as well on how a particular wine is evolving.

All of that said, pursuing perfection is frustrating. There really is no perfect time to drink each bottle. For many wines, the window of enjoyment is stretched over a number of years. The occasion and friends with whom you share a special bottle will no doubt enhance your enjoyment more than choosing the right date to open it.

Ten

WINE PRIMER

I tell people to throw away the vintage charts and invest in a corkscrew. The best way to learn about wine is the drinking.
— Alexis Lichine

Each and every critic judges on a scale envisioned in their minds, based on the parameters that are important to them. It wouldn't be surprising to see French critics embracing acidity, balance, and age-ability, while some American critics are embracing gobs of fresh fruit and power. There are cultural differences that influence these judgments, and, yes, there are the personal preferences of every writer, critic, and professional wine judge.

At a previous Sonoma County Harvest Fair, four of the five judges on our panel were united in our appraisal of wine number 82. To us, it was the best of the group, and we wanted to give it our Best of Class Award, meaning the best of all 82 wines in the "Chardonnay $20 and Over" category. One panel member judged, gnashed his teeth, and argued vehemently against selecting this wine for the coveted award. In the end, out-voted, he made it clear that he would tell all concerned with the competition that he voted against this wine as it was obviously unworthy in his eyes. The Chardonnay we put forward as best, went on to compete against eight other white wines from eight other classes, and the full group of twenty judges selected it as the best white wine of over 200 white wines submitted.

I relate this example not to say the disagreeable judge was wrong and the rest of us were right, but rather to say that it's easy for any knowledgeable person to think they have a lock on what is good. *And nobody does.* It's important to beware of worshipping any one expert's opinion, as writers and judges often stumble on their culture, personal prejudices, and breadth of experience.

You have to find your own way. But if on the journey, you find an expert whose opinions are in sync with yours, that's a bonus.

All of this is a long way of saying that I did not channel my list of favorite wineries from the mouth of God. It limps forth with the biases, tastes, and the favorable experiences I've acquired while traveling and studying wine. It's a short list of some of the producers who have sparked a fire for me: wineries whose creations I've enjoyed over time in Northern California and Europe. It's a sin to exclude the rest of America and most of the Southern Hemisphere, yet one has to draw some sort of line in such a small book. As most of my focus is in Northern California and Europe, I think it best to concentrate on these two areas.

The following recommendations are meant as a starting point for further exploration in each of the seven styles of wine discussed in Chapter One, plus an added style of red wine and two styles of sparkling. This list includes all price ranges. Focus on the wine styles that you like best, try more and more wines in the categories, and in turn build your own list of favorites.

Woven into this resource is a primer on the grapes that make most of the wines you'll encounter. Yet, just as Hunt's and Heinz both make ketchup (or is that catsup?), the two don't taste the same, and two Rieslings can taste dramatically different, from bone dry to syrupy sweet.

So use the list below to get a sense of what styles of wine the grapes generally fall into and to pick up some clues to foods that will enhance them.

DRY SPARKLING

If you enjoy the crisp sensation of Roederer Estate Brut or Mumm Cuvée Napa Brut, you might venture into other wines from the same producers. Roederer Estate's first winemaker, Michel Salgues, French-born and trained, proved that first-class bubbly could be made in the New World, especially in the California vineyards of Mendocino's Anderson Valley. In the tradition of rosé Champagne, Roederer produces a bone dry, pink bubbly that's just beautiful to look at. For more complexity and grander occasions, their L'Ermitage is stunning.

Moving south to Sonoma County, J is earning kudos and Gloria Ferrer is frequently acknowledged for its dry, yet fruity Blanc de Noirs. Domaine Carneros in Napa's portion of the Carneros viticultural area is a rising star. Its top wine, Le Rêve, frequently bests Dom Pérignon in blind tastings in my wine classes. Its 1998 Brut recently bested other California sparklers, which sell for twice its price, at the San Francisco Chronicle Wine Competition.

Across the Atlantic, my favorite values from Champagne have included the sparklers of Pierre Moncuit, Nicolas Feuillatte, and Bollinger. When price is no object, my taste gravitates to Salon for racy acidity and to Krug's Grande Cuvée and Laurent-Perrier's Grand Siècle 'La Cuvée' for multivintage show stoppers and a wealth of complex flavors.

SWEET SPARKLING

I've had good success with Moscato d'Asti from La Spinetta, Cascina Castle't, Ceretto's Santo Stefano, and Bera while other Moscatos may be easier to find. There isn't a huge amount of these Piedmontese wines available in America. As a fall-back, one can always find Asti from the large producers Cinzano and Martini & Rossi. Though these wines are not as delicate, they are much closer to Moscato d'Asti than any of the dry sparklers mentioned above.

A few wineries, like Bonny Doon in California, are making luscious, fruit-driven, sweet sparkling. Again, production is tiny for a nationwide thirst.

VERY DRY WHITE

Frequently bone-dry, Sauvignon Blanc can smell grassy and highly citric, like cutting open a fresh grapefruit. While many wineries opt for the crisp and fruit-driven style, others add the full-flavored richness of butter and oak. The mention on the back label of "malolactic fermentation" and "extended aging in new oak barrels" are clues to these richer styles. Many of us in California enjoy the way the former expression of Sauvignon can be a foil to rich sauces based on butter and cream.

Some of my favorites have been Dry Creek Vineyard, especially their DCV3, White Oak, and Rochioli—all from Sonoma County's respected Dry Creek and Russian River Valleys. Over in the Napa Valley, Honig, Mason, and Voss have been perennial hits at my winetasting events.

White wines from the French appellations Sancerre and Pouilly-Fumé are made from Sauvignon Blanc and most often are super dry and mineral rich. Jean Reverdy, Vacheron, and André Vatan from Sancerre have been particularly good and available.

In the Southern Hemisphere I'm a big fan of the Sauvignons from South Africa's Mulderbosch and Thelema. I also have to mention New Zealand for their aggressive Sauvignons and the bold statement they are making with screw-cap bottles. With no risk of cork taint, the assertiveness of affordable Sauvignon Blanc shines from producers like Lawson's Dry Hills.

Equally adventurous with screw-cap bottles in California is Murphy-Goode's Tin Roof Sauvignon Blanc.

MORE VERY DRY WHITES

GRAPE	COMMENTS	FAVORITES
ROUSSANNE	*This grape from France's Rhône Valley produces aromatic wines with refreshing acidity.*	*Sobon Estate in the Sierra Foothills' Shenandoah Valley*
MARSANNE	*Just as the Sémillon grape adds weight to Sauvignon Blanc, Marsanne is frequently paired up with Roussanne to make blended white wines in the Rhône and California. Wines made from Marsanne can have aromas of nuts and vegetables and show a softer acidity than Roussanne.*	*Rosenblum Cellars*
PINOT GRIGIO	*Going by the alias Pinot Gris, Pinot Grigio runs in style from light and crisp to rich and spicy. Like Riesling, it can be a perfect accompaniment to Thai cuisine in its richer versions.*	*Favorites in the crisp Grigio incarnation are Pepi and Swanson. Richer favorites include J and Montevina in California and Domaine Weinbach and Ernest Burn from Alsace, France.*
VERNACCIA	*The wines of San Gimignano in Tuscany are made from the Vernaccia grape. They are bone dry, mineral rich, and often reminiscent of our own Sauvignon Blanc.*	*Teruzzi & Puthod and San Quirico*

MORE VERY DRY WHITES

GRAPE	COMMENTS	FAVORITES
MALVASIA BIANCA	*This grape produces very aromatic whites, light in body and often quite crisp. It plays a role in Tuscany and stars under the name Malmsey in the production of sweet wines in Madeira.*	*Favorite crisp renditions in California: Wild Horse and Bonny Doon*
ARNEIS	*A native of Piedmont, Arneis is often crisp with flavors of pears and almonds.*	*Seghesio (California) and Ceretto (Piedmont)*
ALBARIÑO	*In Spain, the white wines made from Albariño in Rías Baixas are crisp and fruity.*	*Pazo de Señorans and Martin Codax from Spain and Havens from California*
PALOMINO	*In the south of Spain, the wines of Jerez—Sherry as we call it—can be dry or sweet. The driest will test your mettle as candidates for the driest of dry wines. We don't hear much about Palomino in the United States, but it is the backbone of Sherry production. The wines labeled Fino or Manzanilla are clear and bone dry.*	*Lustau*

RICH WHITE

Sometimes tart like a green apple, Chardonnay achieves great popularity when it tastes of warm weather fruits like pineapple and mango. With a kiss of oak and a dab of butter, the wine can become quite rich and mouth filling. As such, it rides the cusp between very dry whites and rich whites, depending on the sentiments of the producer.

In the northern reaches of Burgundy, Chardonnay is the grape that makes Chablis—a wine that is often the driest expression of Chardonnay—absolutely thirst quenching. Billaud-Simon, Vincent Dauvissat, Verget, and Pascal Bouchard are personal favorites. Likewise, a small number of producers in California are adopting this racier expression of Chardonnay. Most notably, the new winery Roshambo dazzled us at the Sonoma County Harvest Fair with its Imago Chardonnay. Hanzell in Sonoma Valley is another winery embracing this way with Chardonnay, as well as the Anderson Valley bottling from Handley.

Chardonnay has been the workhorse of richly flavored still white wine in California. Many producers treat it to the enriching effects of malolactic fermentation to soften its edges and create a buttery taste. Others add new oak as well, to lend the sweet oak and vanilla character that so many people love. Some even leave a bit of residual sugar in the wine to round it out even more, without saying a word. Favorites: Kunde, MacRostie, Solitude, Beringer, Rombauer, and Cambria.

South of Chablis, again in Burgundy, the wines of Merlin and, for a splurge, Pierre Morey show off the richness of Chardonnay with more structure.

MORE RICH WHITES

GRAPE	COMMENTS	FAVORITES
SÉMILLON	*Possessing an almost unctuous texture, the thick quality of Sémillon makes a great partner to the acidity of Sauvignon Blanc. The two grapes often team up to produce extraordinary dessert wines that hit high notes with fruit tarts and crème caramel.*	*St. Supéry and Chatom Vineyards. For a more crisp style, Stryker in Sonoma's Alexander Valley makes a limited amount.*
VIOGNIER	*This wine combines exotic, perfumed aromas with a scent of peaches and cream. The alcohol level is often as high as or higher than California Chardonnay, creating a full-flavored wine that gives an impression of sweetness.*	*Pride, Rosenblum, Gregory Graham, and organic star Bonterra. In France's Rhône Valley, the appellation of Condrieu is famous for its expensive Viognier. Favorite: Georges Vernay.*
PINOT BLANC	*In Alsace they call it Pinot Blanc and in Italy they call it Pinot Bianco. In California, much of what we call Pinot Blanc is actually the Melon of the Loire Valley. I'm confused too! In any case, styles run from delicate and rounded to rich Chardonnay knock-offs.*	*My favorite, Marcel Deiss, is from Alsace.*

LIGHTLY SWEET WHITE

Riesling reminds me of peaches and limes wrapped in candy with a bouquet of flowers. Often light in body, this wine shines with the diverse flavors in a nibble of sushi.

Check the labels carefully. Many of the great producers of Riesling will make a range of wines each year, from bone dry to super sweet. Look for back and front label details as to the flavor you might expect.

In Germany, the Rieslings labeled Trocken can be shockingly dry, making a dry California Sauvignon Blanc appear more fruity. Little is exported to the United States, but when you find them, they are a good bet to be the driest of Riesling.

Look for German Riesling from the Mosel-Saar-Ruwer: Selbach-Oster, Dr. Loosen, S.A. Prüm, and Kerpen. In the Rheingau, look for Robert Weil and in the Rheinhessen look for Gunderloch. For a great California Riesling, check out Navarro.

MORE LIGHTLY SWEET WHITES

GRAPE	COMMENTS	FAVORITES
GEWÜRZTRAMINER	*Like Riesling, Gewürz, as it's often called, is made in both dry and sweet styles. Often it is full-bodied and reminds me of the taste of fresh lichee and the perfume of roses.*	*Navarro in the Anderson Valley and Domaine Weinbach make great Gewürz across the stylistic landscape. Other favorites include: Claiborne & Churchill and, for more sweetness, widely available Thomas Fogarty and Fetzer.*

MORE LIGHTLY SWEET WHITES

GRAPE	COMMENTS	FAVORITES
MUSCAT	*The grapy, orange blossom scent of Muscat is easy to remember after only one whiff. Most of the wines range from sweet to intensely sweet and make a lovely complement to fresh berries on a summer evening.*	*Two favorites from the Anderson Valley: Husch for sweet Muscat and Navarro for dry.*
CHENIN BLANC	*Chenin is frequently made in an off-dry style, riding the cusp between dry and sweet wine. With aromas of melons, musk, and honey, its acidity acts as the balance to keep any sweetness from tasting cloying.*	*In increasing sweetness, Navarro, Dry Creek, and Beringer Chenin Blanc from California. From France, look for Domaine des Baumard making Chenin in styles from bone dry to dessert.*

LIGHT AND SOFT RED

In France, Gamay, grown in the appellation of Beaujolais, produces juicy, fruity red wines. The lightest versions are often served chilled and taken on picnics. Much of the Gamay planted in California is not Gamay at all. Some has been found to be a clone of Pinot Noir, while others are actually Valdiguié from southwest France. In any case the wines are created as fruit personified, light and juicy. Well done in California is the Valdiguié from J. Lohr.

LIGHT AND SOFT RED

GRAPE	COMMENTS	FAVORITES
PINOT NOIR	*Sometimes Pinot captures the essence of cherries and raspberries. Winemakers often accent these flavors with the brown spice and vanilla of new oak barrels. This often lighter-bodied wine has become a popular red wine to pair with grilled salmon, and its heavier and acidic versions cut through the richness of pâté.*	*In California, try Russian Hill, La Crema, David Bruce, and for a splurge, Williams Selyem. While in France's Burgundy my favorites are Georges Roumier, Domaine Bertagna, and Anne Gros.*
PINOT MEUNIER	*It's like Pinot Noir in a softer way. Lots of Pinot Meunier is grown in the north of France to make Champagne and a few producers have embraced it here as well.*	*Domaine Chandon*
GRIGNOLINO	*This Piedmontese grape produces floral and very light-bodied red wines that some describe as a red Gewürztraminer.*	*Heitz Cellar in the Napa Valley.*
MERLOT	*The darling of many red wine drinkers, Merlot's supple tannins, low acidity, and plum-like fruit make it easy to love and easy to drink in the absence of food. That said, more structured versions are produced that stand up straight and marry well with food.*	*Blackstone, Shafer, and White Oak —all from California.*

Noticeably Acidic Red

I've added this category to the original seven to focus on a crossover area of red wine production. These wines can range from soft-feeling and light-bodied to quite heavy, yet what characterizes them most is a zip that comes from their palpable acidity. They have a refreshing quality as found in a crisp Sauvignon Blanc.

GRAPE	COMMENTS	FAVORITES
SANGIOVESE	*The star of Chianti, Sangiovese can be delicate in color yet lively with acidity, making it a great partner with marinara sauce. Many of Tuscany's greatest wines feature a marriage of Sangiovese and Cabernet Sauvignon.*	*From California: Camellia Cellars, Noceto, Trentadue, and Pietra Santa. From Tuscany: Castello di Fonterutoli, Badia a Coltibuono, Poliziano, Siro Pacenti, and Il Marroneto.*
BARBERA	*Prized for its acidity, Barbera often reminds me of the brightness of fresh blueberries with the darkness of tar. The wines can be quite deeply colored, and like Sangiovese, they won't give out in the presence of tomatoes or spicy sausage.*	*From California: Easton, Jeff Runquist, and Valley of the Moon In Italy, look for La Spinetta and, for value, Michele Chiarlo.*
CORVINA	*Corvina, a grape of which we see little by name, is the star behind the famous wine of Italy's Veneto, Valpolicella. Like Barbera, the wines are lighter in tannin but bracing with acidity. It is also made into heavier dry versions called Amarone and sweet versions called Recioto.*	*Allegrini, Tommaso Bussola, and Masi*

HEAVIER STRUCTURED RED

In its greener versions, Cabernet Sauvignon gives a scent of fresh tobacco. In its ripest renditions, the fruit flavors become almost like berry liqueur. The thick-skinned berries of Cabernet can produce tannic wines that age well. In the younger years, such tannic wines cry out for protein-rich foods to tame them.

California's Cabernet Sauvignon is delicious, especially from the famous Napa Valley. My favorites include: Stag's Leap Wine Cellars, Niebaum-Coppola's Rubicon, Turnbull, Staglin, von Strasser, and Pine Ridge. In the Alexander Valley, look for Stuhlmuller.

Cabernet plays a lead role in these Bordeaux favorites that have some price reasonability: Léoville Las Cases and Léoville Barton.

MORE HEAVIER STRUCTURED REDS

GRAPE	COMMENTS	FAVORITES
CABERNET FRANC	One of Cabernet Sauvignon's parents, Cab Franc often has a pleasant, herbaceous quality about it, with frequently lower tannin levels than its progeny. This leaner member of the family can actually smell like pencil lead and flowers. Go figure.	Favorites from France's famous appellation Chinon in the Loire Valley: Bernard Baudry and Couly-Dutheil.
MALBEC	There's loads of Malbec planted in Argentina, and we see it included in some of the Bordeaux-style blends of California. It can taste softer and more round than lead actor Cabernet Sauvignon.	Imagery Estate in the Sonoma Valley.
PETIT VERDOT	Like Petite Sirah, this wine has great depth of coloration and can be quite tannic. It often adds substance to a Bordeaux-style blend.	Murphy-Goode and Geyser Peak in California.

MORE HEAVIER STRUCTURED REDS

GRAPE	COMMENTS	FAVORITES
MOURVÈDRE	Mourvèdre, a.k.a. Mataro and Monastrell, is a grape that adds the structure of acidity and tannin to lots of Rhône-style blends. When bottled solo, it makes a wine that stands up well to meats garnished in acidic sauces.	Crane Canyon, Cline, Preston, Bonny Doon, and firm blends from Tablas Creek. From Provence: Château de Pibarnon, Domaine Bunan, including their Château La Rouvière.
SYRAH	Syrah is for many the most flavorful grape of the Rhône. One of the hottest wines today, Syrah has flavors ranging from earth to gamey meat to black pepper spice to jammy bombs of fruit. This diversity of flavors has delighted consumers in Europe and the New World, with wines ranging from light to densely packed with flavor. Meat stews often pair well with this complex wine, which also travels by the name Shiraz.	California Favorites: Hamel, Cline, Christopher Creek, Russian Hill, and Rosenblum. Favorites from France's northern Rhône: Guigal and their Château d'Ampuis, Jean-Luc Colombo, and Domaine Combier.
PETITE SIRAH	Certainly not petite, yet related to Syrah, this wine is often the most dense, inky, and tannic of our wines in California. Many winemakers blend it with Zinfandel, making a more complete package of flavors.	Edmeades, Bogle, and Guenoc

More Heavier Structured Reds

Grape	Comments	Favorites
GRENACHE	*Like Syrah, Grenache was made famous in France's Rhône Valley, particularly in Châteauneuf-du-Pape. Some vintners opt for a juicy-fruity style, while most go for full-body. This grape can add alcohol as well as spiciness and strawberry fruit, creating many famous Rhône and Rhône-style blends. In Spain, this grape is known as Garnacha and makes powerful wines in Priorat.*	*Some favorites whose prices have some sanity: Unti in Dry Creek Valley and Domaine de Beaurenard and Château de Beaucastel from Châteauneuf-du-Pape.*
CARIGNANE	*This wine can be quite dense, especially from some of California's old plantings. Its tannins can take time to tame, and, thus, it pairs best in youth with cheeses like Cheddar.*	*Preston and Jessie's Grove in California*
ZINFANDEL	*Zin shines in so many viticultural areas in California. It is made light and fruity for pizza as well as big and alcoholic for anything on the barbecue. Some fans like its jammy incarnations best with bittersweet chocolate, while others favor its late-harvest renditions after dinner with Stilton. Most seem to prefer them big and bursting with fruit.*	*Rosenblum, Zoom, Hartford Family, Ridge, Michael & David Vineyards, Grands Amis, Ravenswood, and Sobon Estate*

MORE HEAVIER STRUCTURED REDS

GRAPE	COMMENTS	FAVORITES
DOLCETTO	Like Barbera, Dolcetto hails from Piedmont in northwest Italy. Though softer in acidity than Barbera, it can be more tannic and quite fruity.	Cosentino and Pietra Santa
NEBBIOLO	This grape produces deep and demanding wines with full-on tannin, acid, and general depth of flavor. The wines can age for many years, and the grape is one of the hardest to grow. The reigning king of Piedmont, Nebbiolo, has been tough to handle in California.	Venture to the northwest of Italy to taste some of the tannic and pricey wines of these favorite producers: Paitin, Paolo Scavino, and La Spinetta.
TEMPRANILLO	This star of Spanish winemaking makes long-lasting wines. The flavors are hard to get a handle on, as this wine has long been associated with a sweetness of oak flavors that can dominate the fruit. Yet with roast lamb, there may be no better choice.	From California: Pagor and Stevenot. From Spain: the wines of Alejandro Fernández and Abadía Retuerta.

DESSERT WHITE

Most of the producers listed in the "Lightly Sweet White" section also make the ultimate in dessert wines—sticky sweet gems that can be dessert in themselves or pair well with most fruit and creamy baked desserts. Navarro is a leader in this respect from California. Greenwood Ridge makes a delicious late-harvest Riesling and the recommended German producers are hard to beat.

Venturing further into Europe, Loire Valley wines, like the sweet Vouvray of Huet and Quarts de Chaume from Domaine des Baumard, can be stunning, as can the luscious, but often richly priced, wines of Sauternes.

If you're adventurous, try some dessert whites from Canada. Two of my favorite wineries are Tinhorn Creek and Inniskillin.

DESSERT RED

Sweet reds come basically in two forms: non-fortified and fortified. The non-fortifieds are late harvest wines made from black grapes. Some of the sugar is not converted to alcohol, leaving natural sweetness. Producers like Rosenblum have taken this approach with Zinfandel and dark Muscat grapes, as has Cline Cellars with their late harvest Mourvèdre.

The other way to go is fortification: adding a shot of high proof alcohol to kill the yeast in the midst of their work, which stops a wine's fermentation short. This creates a naturally sweet wine with higher alcohol, typically in the range between 18 and 20 percent. The legendary wines of Portugal, Port, are made this way, and the weight of these wines makes them a natural with all things chocolate. Explore the broad range of these wines from Taylor Fladgate and Fonseca.

In California, a number of wineries create delicious Port-style wines using Zinfandel, Cabernet Sauvignon, Petite Sirah, and other grapes, often indicating them on the label. Favorites for me have been the Zinfandel Port from Rosenblum, Loxton Cellars Port made from Syrah, a Cabernet-based wine called Obtuse made by Justin, the adventurous Grignolino Port made by Heitz Cellars, and the Vintage Port of St. Amant.

If you're venturing into France for a taste of fortified red wines, try the wines of two appellations in France's south, Maury and Banyuls. From Maury, the wines of Mas Amiel are affordable and delicious. From Banyuls, try Domaine La Tour Vieille and Domaine de La Rectorie.

DRY VS. SWEET

If you found that you came out firmly on one side or the other of the dry-versus-sweet wine divide, remember that there is a role for every type of wine to play, depending on the people and the food involved.

There is a myth in the wine world that appreciation of dry wine equals sophistication. Don't believe it.

Like many before me, I fell in love first with sweet wine. Then came the pseudo-graduation to dry wine, achieving alleged sophistication. Luckily, I got over it, as do many people who reach stage three—a full embracing love affair with sweet wine, dry wine, and all points between.

So if you love wine on the sweet side, don't let any alleged connoisseur label you unsophisticated. Or let them talk, and inwardly wink, knowing that the great sweet wines of the world are often hard to produce and their quantities of production are tiny. Many of these wines are dessert in themselves.

Eleven

RESOURCES

Wine is like sex: few men will admit not knowing all about it!
— Attributed to Hugh Johnson

WINERIES

Many of the world's wine regions are beautiful places to visit: not too hot, not too cold, but just right. And where there's wine, there's food. Visiting a winery and its vineyards is a great way to learn about wine. It's hard to top the experience of standing on a steep hill in the Mosel, taking in the landscape; dining by the sea in Provence, drinking a bottle of wine from a winery you visited earlier that day; or tasting some freshly crushed Chardonnay juice that you helped harvest on a warm autumn day in Sonoma's Russian River. Where I live in Sonoma County, there are trade groups like the Russian River Wine Road that frequently sponsor fun and educational winetastings across a host of member wineries.

Classes

Take a wine class. The great secret about most wine classes is that it's an economical way to taste a boatload of wine. At the Santa Rosa Junior College where I teach, students can taste about 100 different wines in an eight-session class for less than $100. Now not all classes are such a deal, but even at ten times the price, it's much cheaper than buying all of those bottles yourself.

Make Wine

Even if you don't live in a famous wine region, you can make wine at home. I saw this in the rain forest of northern Vancouver Island where a B&B owner, passionate about wine, was making some at home. Start with the grapes, juice, or concentrate (whatever you have available) and find a source for supplies and equipment. Many of the shops that sell home brewing supplies do double duty and handle winemaking products as well.

Work at a Winery

Many wineries need a hand on weekends when most folks are visiting. Pouring in the tasting room is a great opportunity to see the unglamorous side of the wine business. It's work. That said, if you like talking with the public and have an unquenchable passion for wine, you might use this experience as a stepping stone further into the business.

Publications

If I'm really jazzed about a new wine, I like to get a picture of where it comes from. There are a few books that bring together maps of the world's wine regions, and the best is the *Fifth Edition of The World Atlas of Wine* by Hugh Johnson and Jancis Robinson. If you're looking for large maps to display or hang on the wall, Vestra (www.vestra.com) produces detailed and colorful maps of most of the viticultural areas of the West Coast.

For an in-depth reference book, something like an encyclopedia is helpful. The *Oxford Companion to Wine* is incredibly comprehensive and heavy. Also going into depth, but with more pictures and a livelier approach, is *The New Sotheby's Wine Encyclopedia* by Tom Stevenson.

If you're on a budget, the most comprehensive book on wine for $20 is *The Wine Bible* by Karen MacNeil. The book is just loaded with info and is written in a friendly, prosaic style.

Can't find a book at your local retailer? Contact the Wine Appreciation Guild (www.wineappreciation.com). They're a great resource for wine books and accessories. While supplying the wine industry and trade, they also sell direct to consumers.

NEWSPAPERS

It seems that just about every newspaper in the world has or is planning a wine column. *The Wall Street Journal* has become a leader on the national scene. Your local paper may prove most useful if they are featuring wines that are available where you live.

MAGAZINES

If you're more of a foodie than an oenophile, most of the periodicals focusing on food feature at least one article on wine each issue. And many regional magazines, like *Sunset*, report on wine regularly.

If you're ready to go deep, *Wine Spectator, Wine & Spirits*, and *Wine Enthusiast* are most popular in the United States. For me, I prefer the reporting, especially on American wine, that one sees in the English magazines, *Decanter* and *Wine International*. *Wine X* magazine has a very hip approach to wine reporting that has been embraced by a new generation of wine aficionados.

NEWSLETTERS

Are you a fan of a particular winery? Ask about their newsletter: they probably have one. It's a great way to keep up with their latest releases and the special events that you might enjoy attending. Often these provide the most intimate views and learning experiences at a winery, as well as the opportunity to purchase wines before they are released to the larger public.

Many wine retailers have a free newsletter, whether in print or via e-mail. The newsletters help me to plan my purchases before going into the store and alert me to the wines on promotion. And you needn't limit yourself to the local shops. If you live in a state that allows wine to be shipped from out of state, the sky's the limit. This can increase your access to wines that may not be allocated in large numbers to the region where you live.

Good examples can be had with four California wine retailers:

1. K & L Wine Merchants (www.klwines.com)
    They hit the perfect combo of low prices and concise information, and their expert staff has been consistently helpful to me over the years.
2. Traverso's (www.traversos.com)
    Their e-mail newsletter will alert you to allocations of hard-to-find wines before they hit the retail shelf. Their staff exemplifies a Nordstrom-style of customer service.
3. Bottle Barn (www.bottlebarn.com)
    Their newsletter is available in hard copy by mail and by e-mail on request. This Santa Rosa shop has an extensive inventory and truly rock-bottom prices.
4. Beverages & more! (www.bevmo.com)
    Their wine guru often recaps the major wine competition results and places the stars on sale. They also carry a vast selection of beer and spirits.

WORLD WIDE WEB

I must confess that Google is my mainstay for researching wine on the Internet. It leads me often to the winery, where I can download a tech sheet or obtain some background on the vineyards. This may be especially useful if I want to get a preview of how sweet a wine might be and whether the flavor profile will tickle my taste buds.

More importers are maintaining consumer-friendly Web sites that provide background on the wines they are bringing to the United States. A great example is North Berkeley Imports (www.northberkeleyimports.com). With exhaustive profiles of the wineries they represent, North Berkeley educates while it sells.

Retailers are also posting more educational material online. Weimax Wine & Spirits (www.weimax.com) is a California retailer that is not afraid to voice its own opinions: Their winery profiles are frank and educational.

Wine-related trade organizations are providing more consumer information online. Groups like the Russian River Wine Road (www.wineroad.com) post winery and travel information for visitors to Sonoma County. Many groups provide great maps online and by mail, which make a huge difference in traveling the wine country.

Other groups, like the Sonoma County Grape Growers Association (www.scgga.org), while again industry-focused, reach out to consumers with maps and descriptions of local appellations. The same is true with the winery associations like the Sonoma County Wineries Association (www.sonomawine.com), which provide historical as well as practical information about Sonoma wine.

Other useful Web sites include:

- *Decanter* (www.decanter.com)
  This magazine has a brilliant Web site with news and information about wine around the world.
- *Wine Anorak* (www.wineanorak.com)
  This site is another excellent and independent view on the world of wine.
- *Cephas Picture Library* (www.cephas.co.uk)
  Cephas maintains a beautiful collection of wine and related photographs.

- *Local Wine Events* (www.localwineevents.com)
  Eric Orange has amassed a tremendous posting of current and future wine events that spans wineries, retail shops, and tastings at more diverse venues.
- *Winejudging.com* (www.winejudging.com)
  This site provides extensive information about the San Francisco Chronicle Wine Competition and its annual results. I've worked on the competition for a number of years, and the site helps describe some of the scene behind a professional wine competition.
- *Wine Business Online* (www.winebusiness.com)
  From *Wine Business Monthly*, this site provides news for professionals in the wine industry and a useful inside look at the industry's perspective on wine.
- *Wine Institute* (www.wineinstitute.org)
  This California trade organization provides access to research, statistics, wine law, and loads of valuable links.
- *National Agricultural Statistics Service*
  (www.usda.gov/nass)
  As part of the U.S. Department of Agriculture, this service provides volumes of statistics online regarding grape growing and wine production.
- *Alcohol and Tobacco Tax and Trade Bureau* (www.ttb.gov)
  This newly created morph of the BATF is the final source for the excruciating details of U.S. wine law.

RECORDS

Keeping some notes on the wines you like builds a valuable, personal resource. Use something like we suggested in Chapter One, the last few pages of this book, or just keep a list of your favorites on an index card. It helps immensely and creates touchstones for the memories of the people and places where you shared those bottles.

Build Your List of Favorites

Record some notes on the wines you taste. A sample entry might look like this:

2003 Windsor Vineyards
Alexander Valley Gewurztraminer.

Pretty smell of flowers, hint of sweetness,
mouthful of flavors and long acidity. Love it! $10

_____

_____

_____

_____

_____

_____

_____

_____

_____

_____

_____

_____

_____

_____

_____

_____

MY LIST OF FAVORITES

_____

_____

_____

_____

_____

_____

_____

_____

_____

_____

_____

_____

_____

_____

_____

_____

_____

_____

_____

_____